LOST RAILWAYS
OF
NOTTINGHAMSHIRE

G000240887

Geoffrey Kingscott

COUNTRYSIDE BOOKS
NEWBURY, BERKSHIRE

First Published 2004

COUNTRYSIDE BOOKS
3 Catherine Road
Newbury, Berkshire

To view our complete range of books,
please visit us at
www.countrysidebooks.co.uk

ISBN 1 85306 884 5

The cover picture shows a Class B1 61183 with the 3.17 pm
Nottingham–Manchester express leaving Carrington tunnel
on the approach to New Basford station.
(Painting by Colin Doggett from a photo by A. Shaw,
courtesy of Nottingham Central Library Local Studies Library)

Designed by Mon Mohan

Produced through MRM Associates Ltd., Reading
Typeset by Techniset Typesetters, Newton-le-Willows
Printed by Woolnough Bookbinding Ltd., Irthlingborough

CONTENTS

ACKNOWLEDGEMENTS

I have benefited from the advice and assistance of many people in the compiling of this book, ranging from railway experts who have given generously of their time and expertise, to farmworkers who have pointed me in the right direction when I have been in the country looking for traces of old track. I am grateful to all of them.

Nottinghamshire is fortunate in having a number of eminent railway historians, and I have learned to place considerable reliance on works by Colin Aldworth, Jack Cupit, Mac Hawkins, Alfred Henshaw and Michael Vanns, some of whose works are mentioned in the Bibliography. I have received a lot of assistance from historian and former librarian Stephen Best. Dorothy Ritchie, of the local studies section at the Nottingham Central Library, guided me through the library's impressive photographic collection.

Thanks finally must go to my patient wife Judy, who has helped with every aspect of the work, to my brother-in-law Rodger Smith, who accompanied me on many of the site visits and who was always prepared to scramble up embankments or down overgrown cuttings when the need arose, and whose photographs invariably turned out better than mine, and to my young grandchildren, Harry, Emma, Sophie, Jack and Rebecca, who showed admirable fortitude whenever an outing with Granddad turned out to be yet another cross-country trek to find traces of lost railways.

AREA MAP OF NOTTINGHAMSHIRE'S RAILWAYS

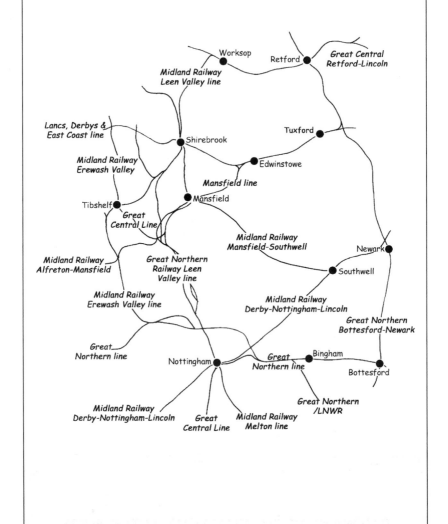

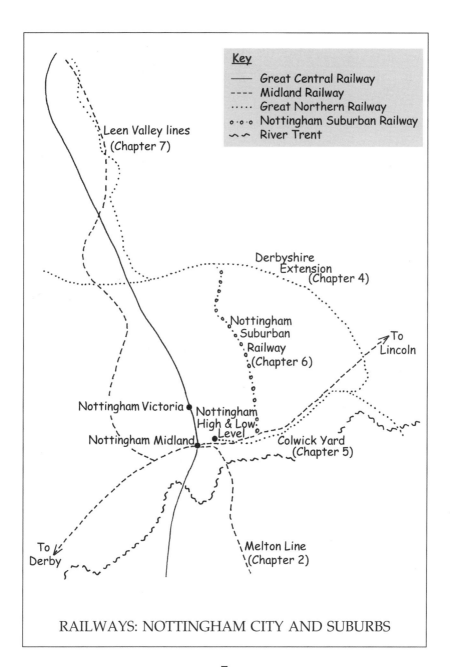

Key

—— Great Central Railway
---- Midland Railway
····· Great Northern Railway
o·o·o Nottingham Suburban Railway
∿∿ River Trent

Leen Valley lines
(Chapter 7)

Derbyshire
Extension
(Chapter 4)

Nottingham
Suburban
Railway
(Chapter 6)

To
Lincoln

Nottingham Victoria
Nottingham
High & Low
Level

Nottingham Midland

Colwick Yard
(Chapter 5)

To
Derby

Melton Line
(Chapter 2)

RAILWAYS: NOTTINGHAM CITY AND SUBURBS

ABBREVIATIONS

The following abbreviations are used in this book:

ANB&EJR	Ambergate, Nottingham, Boston & Eastern Junction Railway
GCR	Great Central Railway
GNR	Great Northern Railway
GWR	Great Western Railway
LD&ECR	Lancashire, Derbyshire & East Coast Railway
LMS	London, Midland & Scottish Railway
LNER	London & North Eastern Railway
LNWR	London & North Western Railway
MR	Midland Railway
MS&LR	Manchester, Sheffield & Lincolnshire Railway
SR	Southern Railway

Introduction

A dotted line on a map alongside those two words 'Dismantled Railway' can conjure up a wide variety of feelings, harking back to a time when the railway system formed the arteries and veins of England, when everyone and everything travelled by train. There were magnificent huge steam locomotives on the crack expresses, or homely little tank engines on the branch lines. Stationmasters, even of village stations, were people of importance.

But how dismantled is 'dismantled'? Will there be simply a piece of crumbling embankment in a farmer's field, or a mass of brambles obscuring and blocking the track? Or will there still be a majestic reminder of the olden days, such as Bennerley viaduct near Ilkeston, going from nowhere to nowhere but dominating the landscape? Or a preserved trackbed, such as that of the former Southwell to Farnsfield line, now designated by Nottinghamshire County Council as a footpath and cycleway?

There are a lot of lost lines in Nottinghamshire. The reasons go back to the fierce rivalry between different railway companies in the 19th century, which created considerable duplication (even triplication!) of services. Sometimes different lines ran parallel and within sight of each other, and there would be rival village stations a few hundred yards apart. When rationalisation came, therefore, there were many lines in the county that could be cut, and were.

In the 19th century Nottinghamshire was fought over by two ambitious and expansionist railway companies. These were the Midland Railway and the Great Northern Railway, and their successors in the 20th century became the London, Midland & Scottish (LMS) and the London & North Eastern Railway (LNER). Much of the history of railways in Nottinghamshire in the Victorian era revolved round the Midland Railway fiercely trying to hold on to its initial

9

'One of the sights of the shires', the coal trains snaking through Nottinghamshire. This one is pictured at Thoresby Colliery Junction. (Henry Priestley, courtesy of Nottingham City Council Leisure and Community Services Central Library Local Studies Library)

monopoly, while the Great Northern kept stretching out its tentacles into Midland territory.

A large part of this rivalry was because of coal. The Nottinghamshire coalfields were among the most productive in the country, and in both the 19th century and the 20th century the nation's industry was highly dependent on coal. 'One of the sights of the shires' was how an observer described the long coal trains snaking down out of Nottinghamshire to distribute their valuable loads to all parts of Britain. Coal was responsible for the railways coming early to the county. So early, in fact, that Nottinghamshire can claim to have originated the concept of trucks running on rails. 'Alonge the passage now laide with Railes' – that single phrase, from a contract of 1604, is the first written evidence of a true railway anywhere in the world.

10

Two hundred years later, after Richard Trevithick had demonstrated his first experimental steam locomotive in 1804, but before the opening of the Stockton to Darlington railway in 1825, another horse-drawn railway was created. This was an 8 mile stretch of line, laid between the important industrial town of Mansfield and the village of Pinxton, which was situated on an arm of the Cromford Canal. This line was again created for the conveyance of coal; and is still in use today.

Every railway company also wanted passengers, however. Even in its horse-drawn days the Mansfield to Pinxton railway had passengers – the enterprising landlord of the Boat Inn at Pinxton ran a weekly passenger coach to Mansfield market and back.

In the long run the Midland Railway and its successors, the LMS and then the London Midland region of British Railways, did hold on to their initial advantages, for the majority of lines still open in Nottinghamshire are former Midland routes. There were some line and station closures in the county as early as the First World War, and still more in the 1920s as trams and buses began to attract commuter passengers from suburban railways. But most of the lost lines described in the following chapters resulted from the closures recommended in the Beeching report of 1963. The lines may have been lost to the actual running of services, however, but they have not been lost to memory.

I assume my readers will have no difficulty with imperial measures (yards and feet rather than metres) – if there is a problem, advice can easily be sought from a member of the older generation! Throughout the book I have deliberately avoided using any specialised railway terminology. The one exception, too useful to be avoided, is 'up' and 'down'. To a railwayman an 'up line' is the line which leads to London, and the 'down line' is the one which leads away from London. This is extended to platforms in stations, so that the 'up platform' is where you catch your train towards London, and the 'down platform' the one you use for a train going the other way.

The other unavoidable term is 'Grouping'. As the era of railway expansion developed, there were many railway companies, some of which were merged into larger companies, and others which changed their names. The two major 19th century companies that figure in this book are the Midland Railway (MR) and the Great Northern Railway (GNR), bitter rivals. At the beginning of the 20th century a third major company drove a new line through Nottinghamshire, the Great Central Railway (GCR).

Despite all the amalgamations, there were still well over 100 railway companies in Britain in 1922. This was a cause of considerable confusion and inefficiency, so the Government forced through what was known as 'Grouping', which took effect on 1st January 1923. Every existing railway company in Britain was forced to join one of four big companies, London, Midland and Scottish (LMS), the London & North Eastern Railway (LNER), the Great Western Railway (GWR) and the Southern Railway (SR). This is when the Midland Railway became part of the LMS and the Great Central and Great Northern part of the LNER – and the rivalry in Nottinghamshire continued until (and some say beyond) nationalisation and the creation of British Railways in 1948!

This book recalls the excitement of the days when the lines were busy with traffic, investigating why and how they closed, and the heritage they left behind. And in Nottinghamshire there is the added excitement of revival, of railways coming into their own again, whether as heritage railways or reopened commuter lines.

Geoffrey Kingscott

1
Pride Of The Shires

The Great Central Railway

In the closing years of the Victorian era, Sir Edward Watkin of the Manchester, Sheffield & Lincolnshire Railway had a vision. He would create a railway for the future. A railway engineered for the 20th century, which would allow expresses to sweep down from Manchester and the Midlands of England to London, then on to a Channel Tunnel and into the mainland of Europe.

Well, the Channel Tunnel did not come in 1881, when construction was actually started, only to be abandoned; or in 1906, when Parliament squashed the idea. As we know, it was not to become a reality until the last decade of the 20th century. But Sir Edward did at least achieve part of his ambition. On 15th March 1899 the section of the line from Annesley in Nottinghamshire to Quainton Road Junction in Buckingham-shire was opened, linking up with existing lines to complete the Manchester to London route. In preparation for this moment, Sir Edward's company was renamed the Great Central Railway.

Faster than the alternative Midland Railway routes to London, and with through coaches to places such as Bournemouth, Swansea or Penzance, the Great Central's crack expresses were much favoured by businessmen. In the major cities on its route, Manchester, Sheffield, Nottingham and Leicester, it engendered immense pride.

And Nottingham's Victoria station was one of the showplaces of Britain's railway system.

Back in 1881 Nottingham was served by two mainline stations, the Midland Railway's station on Station Street, and the Great Northern Railway's station on London Road, both some distance from the centre of the city. In that year Nottingham Corporation came up with a carefully thought-out plan for a new central station serving both companies, and positioned close to the very

13

Nottingham Victoria station in 1907. (Courtesy of Nottingham City Council Leisure and Community Services Central Library Local Studies Library)

PRELIMINARY ANNOUNCEMENT.

Corporation of   Nottingham.

OPENING
OF THE
New Great Central
LINE.

On the Opening Day of the New Railway,

WEDNESDAY, MARCH 15, 1899,

An Employees' Excursion will run to

LONDON

FOR THE DAY AND HALF-DAY.
With Extensions to Eight Days.

From Hucknall, Bulwell Common, New Basford, Carrington, Arkwright Street, and Ruddington.

FARE 4/- (2d. extra charged for expenses.)

Children under 14 Half-Fare.

Bills announcing times of departure, and Tickets, will be ready in a few days.

AS THE NUMBER OF TICKETS ARE STRICTLY LIMITED EARLY APPLICATION MUST BE MADE.

Applications for Saloons and Engaged Compartments to be made at once to Mr. C. ___ ROYD, Weights and Measures Office.

The Nottingham Corporation supported the new Great Central line. This handbill announces a special excursion for their employees, even before the new Victoria station had been completed. (Courtesy of Nottingham City Council Leisure and Community Services Central Library Local Studies Library)

The frontage of Nottingham Victoria station in 1930. (Courtesy of Nottingham City Council Leisure and Community Services Central Library Local Studies Library)

centre of the city. But the rivalry between the Midland and the Great Northern was too great for them to agree to share premises.

However, the idea did not go away, and when the Manchester, Sheffield & Lincolnshire Railway (shortly to be renamed, as we have noted, the Great Central) revealed its plans for a new main line passing through Nottingham, the notion was revived. The Midland still maintained its haughty refusal to collaborate, but the Great Northern and the MS&LR agreed to work with the city authorities on a brand new station.

And what a station it was!

Superbly engineered, and established close to the commercial heart of the city, no expense was spared in its construction. Designed by a local architect, A.E. Lambert, in what was called the French Renaissance style, it was built in red brick with facings in Darley Dale stone. In the centre of the frontage rose a 100 foot high clock tower, which immediately became a city landmark. The elegant and spacious booking hall had seven ticket windows, three for each of the two companies, and one for excursions. The roof would have done justice to a cathedral. Beneath it a wide lattice footbridge connected the booking hall with the two island platforms, which had double track bays at either end. The refreshment rooms were the last word in late Victorian opulence. A tunnel beneath the platforms, equipped with the latest in hydraulic lifts, allowed station staff to move parcels and luggage easily and quickly. The station, the construction cost of which was over a million pounds (an unimaginable sum in those days), was designed to handle 170 passenger trains a day.

There was some argument over what the station should be called. The Great Central wanted the name Nottingham Central, for obvious reasons. The Great Northern, however, thought that would belittle their role, and suggested the rather banal name of Nottingham Joint Station. It was the Town Clerk of Nottingham who pointed out that the scheduled opening day, 24th May 1900, was Queen Victoria's birthday, and suggested Nottingham Victoria as the name. The suggestion was enthusiastically accepted. Poignantly, it turned out to be the old Queen's last birthday, for she died in January 1901.

The Midland Railway just had to compete, and immediately set about building a brand-new station at Carrington Street, just round the corner from its existing site. They engaged the same architect, A.E. Lambert, though the designs were very different. Their new station (still operating today) was completed in 1904. Midland and Victoria were then in direct competition for the London traffic, trying to clip minutes off the times of their prime expresses.

Nottingham Victoria station, and the Great Central line, lasted for 60 years before they both fell victim – to simple economics, according to the planners, but to Midland skulduggery, according to Great Central enthusiasts.

18

Under the 1923 Grouping the Midland Railway had gone on to form the core of the LMS (London, Midland & Scottish), while the Great Central became part of the LNER (London & North Eastern Railway). In fact the LNER did the Great Central proud, and Sir Nigel Gresley's A3 Pacifics, some of the finest and most powerful steam locomotives ever made, were used on the top LNER trains on this line in order to compete with the LMS.

Immediately after the Second World War the LNER invented the term *Master Cutler* for its Sheffield to London Marylebone service. The *Master Cutler* quickly proved a favourite with Nottingham businessmen, for convenience, speed and reliability. Introduced in 1947, it left Sheffield at 7.40 am, with a return service leaving Marylebone at 6.15 pm. Since nationalisation the *Master Cutler* name has continued to be applied to selected trains,

Platform 7 at Nottingham Victoria station, Bank Holiday Monday 1950, with, in the foreground, the Master Cutler train with a Gresley locomotive. (Nottingham Evening Post, courtesy of Nottingham City Council Leisure and Community Services Central Library Local Studies Library)

19

the timings varying over the years, but it has never regained the cachet it had under the LNER.

On railway nationalisation in 1948 the LMS lines became part of the London Midland region, and the LNER lines became part of the Eastern region. The powers-that-be, however, were uneasy at the lack of clear geographical demarcation in the Nottinghamshire area, with London Midland and Eastern region lines criss-crossing each other. Eventually, on 1st February 1958, ten years after nationalisation, administration of the old Great Central line was switched from the Eastern region to the London Midland.

This, the Great Central's partisans allege, was where the skulduggery came in. According to the Great Central people the controllers of the London Midland region still had a pre-nationalisation mindset, and their loyalties were dominated by LMS and even Midland Railway thinking. And once the Great Central was part of their empire they set about running it down.

Well, that is as maybe. It is certain that old railway loyalties have been surprisingly persistent, up to and including the present time. Even today, if you talk to any steam railway enthusiast, you will often find a prejudice in favour of one of the old companies. 'Of course, I'm an LNER man myself' or 'I only collect Midland Railway material; I'm not interested in anything post-Grouping' are examples of remarks made to the author when he was researching this book.

And if anyone thinks that such partiality is limited to conversation among railway buffs, they have only to look at the version of the board game *Monopoly* as sold in the UK. The board, as practically everyone knows, features the principal streets of London, and four railway stations. But there is no mention of London's largest stations – Victoria, Waterloo and Paddington. Instead we have King's Cross, Fenchurch Street, Marylebone and Liverpool Street. And why? The author put the question to Hasbro, the current owners of the *Monopoly* game, but they could not find an answer. Could it be that there was a railway enthusiast at work who unashamedly chose only LNER stations!

But perhaps the accusation of partisanship over the Great Central line was exaggerated. Maybe it was just a question of

Nottingham Victoria station in its later, quieter, days. Sunshine streams through the glass roof creating a dappled effect on the platforms below. (Nottingham Evening Post, courtesy of Nottingham City Council Leisure and Community Services Central Library Local Studies Library)

catchment areas. The Great Central line simply duplicated the Midland lines for Nottingham and the north, but between Nottinghamshire and London the Midland lines passed through important centres of population whereas the Great Central, once south of Leicester, took a much more rural route.

Whatever the merits or demerits of the argument, the London Midland region, as soon as it had taken over the old Great Central line, certainly did drop any pretence at providing competing services on the London expresses. From 3rd January 1960 express trains ran only on the old Midland lines. The Great Central route, it was announced, would be serviced by 'semi-fast' trains. To add insult to injury British Railways put up posters at Nottingham Victoria station telling passengers that the Midland station was the station for 'fast services to London'. Only three services a day would now run in each direction between Nottingham Victoria and London Marylebone, and none provided refreshment facilities.

The next move came in March 1963 when local stations along the line were closed, while cross-country trains were steadily diverted to other routes. All this running-down, it should be noted, was well in progress before the publication (also in 1963) of the Beeching report. If there was a villain in the plot to close the Great Central, for once it was not Dr Beeching.

Most freight on the Great Central was ended in 1963, and on 4th September 1966 all through services came to an end. At a stroke not only did Nottingham Victoria lose its London (Manchester–Marylebone) service, but also the services that ran between York and Poole, York and Bristol, and Sheffield and Swindon. Withdrawn at the same time were two news-paper trains working out of London, and the Nottingham–Marylebone parcels train. The final Great Central train to London was the 5.15 pm from Nottingham on Saturday, 3rd September 1966.

Victoria station became more and more desolate, although, as our photograph shows, all the infrastructure remained in place and was well looked after. For a further twelve months a diesel train continued to run between Nottingham Victoria and Rugby Central, with only Platform 6 in use for this service. Then came the final curtain. It was at 5.34 pm on 2nd September 1967 that

22

A once proud station now deserted. A solitary railwayman, Wilfred Cook, checks his instructions. The year is 1967, and the end is nigh. (Nottingham Evening Post, courtesy of Nottingham City Council Leisure and Community Services Central Library Local Studies Library)

the last passenger train, a diesel unit to Rugby, left Nottingham Victoria station. The start of the Rugby service was moved away from Victoria, to Nottingham's Arkwright Street station. From Arkwright Street it was allowed to continue for another 20 months, before being withdrawn altogether.

So Nottingham's Victoria station, the city's pride and joy, was deserted at last. But its tranquillity did not last long. Within ten days of that final train the demolition contractors had arrived. They worked quickly and effectively, so much so that within six months the vast complex had been completely eradicated, with the exception of the clock tower, which was allowed to remain and continues today as a poignant reminder of the golden age of Nottinghamshire's railways.

The site of Victoria station has been turned into a shopping complex (called the Victoria Centre), car park and block of flats, though even this huge complex could not make full use of the vast cutting that the Victorian engineers had created. A 'hole' remained for many years until finally filled by extensions to the shopping centre.

And what of the Great Central line in Nottinghamshire today? Here there are two different stories. North of the River Trent the line has gone for ever, with practically every trace obliterated. South of the river the trackbed, and some of the rails, are still in place, and there are ambitious plans to reopen the line as a heritage railway.

North of the Trent the line can only be retraced using old maps. The Great Central entered Nottinghamshire between Blackwell and Kirkby-in-Ashfield, and ran through Annesley, Bulwell and Basford to Nottingham. A station, called Kirkby Bentinck (originally Kirkby & Pinxton), was built at Castle Hill, south-west of Kirkby-in-Ashfield, but it was too far from the town to be popular and was closed in March 1963. No trace of it now survives.

A mile or so brought the line to Annesley tunnel, at the south end of which was the Annesley junction with the old Great Northern line. There was a locomotive depot and important sidings at Annesley, which was a major centre for Great Central activity. As there was little in the way of housing in the vicinity of the sidings a shuttle train, the Dido (an acronym for

24

Today the clock tower is the only remnant of Nottingham Victoria station. A shopping centre and a high block of flats now occupy the site. (Rodger Smith)

25

A glimpse across the little-used Hollinwell & Annesley station, looking north across a part of Annesley sidings, 1955. (Henry Priestley, courtesy of Nottingham City Council Leisure and Community Services Central Library Local Studies Library)

'Day In Day Out'), brought railway workers in from Bulwell Common station.

Alas, there is nothing now to show that one of Britain's greatest railways once passed this way. After closure of the Great Central line the embankments were bulldozed into the surrounding fields, cuttings were filled in, and the whole area used for the dumping of colliery waste, later covered by topsoil and grass. Colliery waste was also used to fill the Annesley tunnel and cutting.

The Great Central entered the Nottingham conurbation on the magnificent Bulwell viaduct (44 feet high and 420 yards long), which took the line over the Nottingham to Hucknall trunk road (today the A611), the River Leen, the Midland Railway's Leen Valley line between Nottingham and Mansfield, and the road from Nottingham to Bestwood village. This it did using 26 arches. After closure of the line the viaduct was demolished in stages, but had completely disappeared by the beginning of the 1990s.

The old line continued through the Nottingham suburbs of Bulwell and Basford, but its course has been almost entirely been built over. It then went into the 'rathole', as it was always known, a tunnel whose entrance was near the bridge that carried Arnold Road over the line. After passing through the 665 yard long Sherwood Rise tunnel and a deep cutting that once housed Carrington station (the station closed as early as 1928 as buses took over much of Nottingham's suburban traffic), the line continued into the 1,189 yard Mansfield Road tunnel.

'Through cuttings deep to Nottingham
Precariously we wound;
The swallowing tunnel made the train
Seem London's Underground...'

So had written John Betjeman, the late Poet Laureate who celebrated railways in verse and prose, in a poem entirely devoted to the Great Central Railway (*Great Central Railway, Sheffield Victoria to Banbury*).

Carrington station cutting has been filled in, but the two tunnels are still there, though blocked off, obscured and inaccessible. South from Victoria station the line went through the short Victoria Street tunnel, to emerge again, after this long incarceration in tunnels and cuttings, at Weekday Cross. The Victoria Street tunnel, though not accessible to the public, is today used for steam heating pipes for the Victoria Centre complex.

In order to build Victoria station and this part of the line through the centre of Nottingham as many as 1,300 houses had to be demolished, as well as 20 public houses, a workhouse and a church.

Construction of the mighty Bulwell viaduct nearing completion 1895–1900.
(Newton, courtesy of Leicestershire, Leicester and Rutland Record Office)

Carrington station in its deep cutting, pictured around 1900. (Courtesy of Nottingham City Council Leisure and Community Services Central Library Local Studies Library)

At Weekday Cross the line emerged from tunnels and cuttings on to a viaduct, which was still there until the last years of the 20th century, the only visible part of the Great Central line to survive north of the River Trent. This too has now largely fallen to the demolition squad, apart from the last four arches, which help to carry Nottingham's new tram service (opened in March 2004).

From the viaduct the line moved on to a huge girder bridge that took the track over the Midland station and into Arkwright Street station, and then continued to the River Trent by a viaduct over the Meadows, a low-lying area of Nottingham. The girder bridge, Arkwright Street station, the viaduct and the four-track bridge over the river have all been demolished and the area redeveloped.

However, once south of the river, the prospects for the railway aficionado begin to look up. The route of the line can now be traced, steadily becoming clearer as it moves through the prosperous suburbs of Wilford and West Bridgford. After a short stretch of countryside where the Nottingham conurbation finally comes to an end, the route approaches the village of Ruddington, which once had its own small island station on the line. The station (on the north-western edge of the village), which in the early 1900s had 17 trains a day in each direction on weekdays, was closed to passengers on 4th March 1963. The

The Sherwood Rise tunnel under construction towards the end of the 19th century. (Newton, courtesy of Leicestershire, Leicester and Rutland Record Office)

31

Constructing Nottingham Victoria station. (Courtesy of Nottingham City Council Leisure and Community Services Central Library Local Studies Library)

station buildings and platforms were razed to the ground, and have disappeared without trace, but just south of the village is where a Nottinghamshire section of a revived Great Central Railway is being created.

When the original line was still operating, a branch here led to sidings that served a large military supplies depot at Ruddington. Fortunately, after the abandonment of the depot, the rails were never lifted, but left in situ. The extensive depot site has been turned into Rushcliffe Country Park, with lakes, picnic areas and a network of walks. And the sidings have been converted into the Nottingham Transport Heritage Centre, complete with its own new Ruddington station. This has all the usual appurtenances of steam railway activity – locomotive

The Weekday Cross viaduct when it was still in place. (A. Shaw, courtesy of Nottingham City Council Leisure and Community Services Central Library Local Studies Library)

Four of the arches from the old Great Central viaduct now carry Nottingham's new tram service. (Rodger Smith)

The girder bridge, now demolished, which took the Great Central line over the Nottingham Midland station. A picture taken in 1907. (Courtesy of Nottingham City Council Leisure and Community Services Central Library Local Studies Library)

and carriage workshops, signal boxes and footbridges, and period features. And at weekends a steam locomotive pulls trains on old Great Central tracks to Rushcliffe Halt, about 5 miles to the south.

Four Great Central coaches, of the type known as Barnums, are being restored here. Only 36 of these coaches were ever built, in the period 1910–1911, and they were the first open saloon coaches (as distinct from coaches with separate compartments) in the UK. They were named after Phineas T. Barnum, the great American showman of the period, because their style was thought to be distinctively American.

Ruddington is Nottinghamshire's only piece of heritage railway, and at the time of writing is still a small-scale operation compared with what is happening not far away. Just beyond the county boundaries are two important heritage railway centres. Some 15 miles to the north-west, in Derbyshire, the Midland Railway Centre at Butterley is a growing complex, while 10 miles to the south, at Loughborough in Leicestershire, the Great Central Railway revival is a reality. Regular services, drawn by steam locomotives, run to Leicester from the superbly restored Loughborough Central station, with intermediate stations, also carefully restored, at Quorn and Rothley.

But what is important about the Ruddington activity is that there are long-term plans to link up the Nottingham Railway Heritage Centre with the Loughborough Great Central Railway. The trackbed south of Ruddington, through East Leake to the Leicestershire border, is still intact, though, as our photograph shows, the East Leake station site is derelict. The main problem will be to recreate a demolished bridge, which carried the old GCR line over the Midland main line near Loughborough Midland station.

The latest news was given to the author by John Bryant, membership secretary of the Great Central Railway NDA (Northern Development Association) project, in an email message shortly before this book went to press. 'The long-term aim is to join the two GCRs together via a replacement bridge at Loughborough. The old bridge was demolished in the late 1970s. The current guestimate for this replacement structure is £5 million to £8 million. The GCR Link company is running with

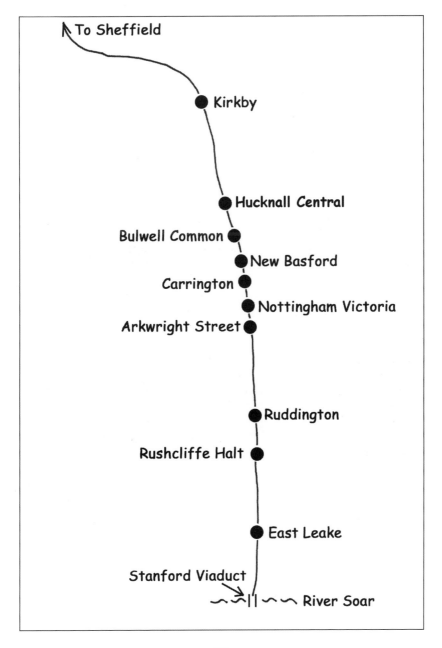

Visitors to the Ruddington Transport Heritage Centre are here seen boarding a train hauled by a steam locomotive for a run along a restored section of the Great Central line. (Rodger Smith)

The little train arriving at Rushcliffe Halt. (Rodger Smith)

East Leake station, south of Ruddington, is derelict, with all the buildings removed, but one set of tracks has been restored. (Author)

However, the nearby Barnstone tunnel is still in excellent condition and the restored single track line runs through it. (Rodger Smith)

The splendid Stanford viaduct over the River Soar. (Author)

this project and needs around £30,000 just to do a new feasibility study combined with an environmental impact study of the proposed works.'

When this plan comes to fruition Ruddington will then become effectively the northern terminus of the restored section of the Great Central railway.

Watching these developments with interest is a Nottingham man, Dave Ablitt, who in the mid-1980s gave himself the unique experience of walking the closed line when much of the infrastructure was still in place. Dave's long walk took him from Annesley to just north of Calvert, close to where the route from Aylesbury to Marylebone station is still a functioning railway. He did it over a period of several months, and took a tape recorder with him, in which he recorded the memories and opinions of

End of the line. Pictured from one mile inside Leicestershire, looking northwards, back towards Nottinghamshire, this is as far as the Nottinghamshire restored section of the original Great Central track runs. The line on the right leads to a later junction with the existing London Midland line. (Author)

41

many of those who had worked on the line or been associated with it. He later wrote these interviews up and today this forms an impressive archive of some 70,000 words, which gives a rounded picture of the Great Central Railway way of life.

2
The Severed Head

The Midland's Alternative Route to London

The three-span bowstring girder bridge which carried the Melton line over the River Trent. Today it is used as a road bridge. However, it is also famous in television history as the bridge Karla (Patrick Stewart) walked over to defect in the spy series 'Smiley's People'. (Rodger Smith)

A man lights a cigarette. It is a signal. On the opposite side of the river the watchers see it, and whisper to one another, but keep very still. Then the man with the cigarette, Karla, one of the key figures in the Soviet Union's spy system, slowly begins to cross the bridge. This is the moment of greatest danger. The bridge is a

43

border crossing, between East and West Germany, the Cold War is at its height, and Karla is defecting.

This was the key scene in the television series *Smiley's People*, made back in 1982. Based on a novel by John le Carré, it is recognised as one of the greatest spy dramas of the 20th century. The series featured a star-studded cast, including Alan Guinness, Alan Bates, Ian Richardson, and Patrick Stewart (who played Karla). The scene was filmed at the Lady Bay bridge in Nottingham, which resembles an actual famous crossing point between East and West Germany. Filming was carried out in the evenings in December 1981, with the road closed to traffic and all the paraphernalia of an East German checkpoint – watchtowers, traffic control posts, warning notices, fences etc – being re-erected each evening by the scene-setters.

Lady Bay bridge is part of another of Nottinghamshire's major lost lines. This time, unusually, it is a former Midland Railway one. Unusually, because the Midland Railway was first into Nottinghamshire, and picked all the best routes, which gave them a good chance of survival when the cutbacks came.

Once the citizens of Nottingham had the choice of three railway routes to London – the Great Central line, or two Midland Railway lines, one through Melton Mowbray and one through Trent Junction. Of these only the latter survives today. It was the original route from Nottingham to London, so Nottingham is back with the Hobson's Choice situation it had between 1840 and 1879.

The original Midland Counties Railway had connected Derby and Nottingham in 1839, and in 1840 had created a line south to Leicester joining the Derby–Nottingham line at the mid-point – Trent Junction. Eventually the line to Leicester pushed further and further south until it reached London. In 1847 the opening of the Erewash Valley line running northwards from Trent Junction fed more traffic through the junction, and created a direct route between London and Scotland.

In the late 1860s there had been a very strong growth in Midland Railway traffic generally, and Trent Junction, which now had its own interchange station, was getting seriously congested. This coincided with an interest in a line down through eastern Leicestershire to link up with the workings of important iron ore deposits near Waltham, which were just starting to be exploited. In 1872 the Midland Railway chairman, W.P. Price, was quoted in *The Times* saying that in the three years 1869–1871 traffic had increased by 'an incredible amount' and that 'it was continuing to increase and had every prospect of increasing in an equally encouraging ratio'.

Something had to be done to alleviate the pressure on Trent Junction. So the most important of the old Midland lines to become a lost railway was created. On 1st November 1879 the Midland Railway opened the line from Nottingham to Melton Mowbray for goods traffic, crossing the River Trent on that three-span bowstring girder bridge and then skirting the famous Trent Bridge cricket ground.

The line opened for passenger services on 2nd February 1880. In the following months the line south from Melton Mowbray was extended to join the main Midland lines, thus enabling the Midland to offer a through London service from Nottingham that was more direct than the service through Trent Junction. The expresses started to run on this route on 1st June 1880. The route was extended northwards by building a link railway connecting two existing Midland Railway lines, the Leen Valley line and the Erewash Valley line. The link went from Radford, west of Nottingham, to Trowell, opening on 1st May 1875.

London was now only 2¼ hours from Nottingham, and with the Settle to Carlisle section (still one of the most dramatic routes on the British railway network) under construction, the Midland was also preparing itself to offer a fast route to Scotland.

To allow expresses to maintain high speeds, the new Nottingham to Melton line was heavily engineered with a minimum gradient. The bridge over the River Trent that we have already mentioned, now the Lady Bay road bridge, was an important construction, consisting of three wrought iron spans of 100 feet each, supported on substantial piers which had been driven deep into the river bed.

There were six local stations along the line, named Edwalton, Plumtree (for a short time known as Plumtree & Keyworth), Widmerpool, Upper Broughton, Old Dalby and Grimston, though some of these were at some distance from the villages after which they were named. The first four stations were in

45

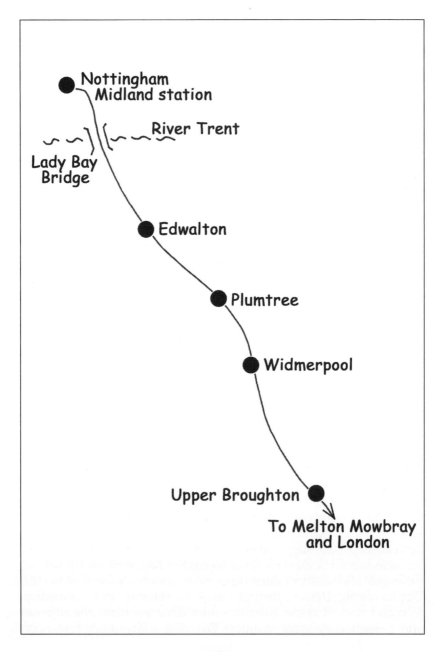

The Edwalton station buildings, pictured in 1949, when the station was no longer used for regular passenger services. (Stations UK, Southport).

Nottinghamshire and the latter two in Leicestershire, and all except Upper Broughton were fitted out with a signal box, goods yard and shed.

By 1904 there were ten stopping trains a day running in each direction, and though these were cut to five as an economy measure during the First World War, the full timetable was restored by 1920.

However, in 1924 there was an ominous development. Daily bus services started running to Edwalton, Plumtree and Keyworth. By 1928 the leading private local bus company, Barton, was running a service every three hours (every hour on Saturdays) between Nottingham and Melton Mowbray, calling at Edwalton, Plumtree, Normanton-on-the-Wolds and Upper Broughton. Another major regional bus company, Midland Red, also ran a service for a time between Nottingham and Leicester, passing through Edwalton, Plumtree, Keyworth

47

and Widmerpool. The advent of the bus services, picking up and setting down in the very centres of the villages they served, cruelly exposed the inconvenient siting of the railway stations on the line.

There was a temporary revival of the railway's fortunes in the Second World War, with severe fuel restrictions on bus services. Old Dalby became particularly busy because of the building of a nearby army camp (later a REME depot). However, it was noticed that there were still very few passengers travelling to and from Edwalton, and the station was closed in July 1941. The closure was intended to be only temporary, 'for the duration' as the phrase was at that time (meaning for the duration of the national emergency caused by the war), but in fact it was never to reopen as a fully functioning passenger station although there was a temporary reopening in 1947 when road transport in the area was disrupted by widespread flooding. Also as a wartime measure, staff reductions were made at Upper Broughton station, which meant it could open for only three short periods in each day, and this arrangement continued after the war was over.

The bus companies were able to reinstate and even expand their services to the villages served by the Nottingham–Melton line after the war, offering fares that were well under those charged by the railways. The village stations were now obviously uneconomic. Upper Broughton closed in May 1948, and Plumtree and Widmerpool lost their passenger services (remaining open only for limited goods traffic) in February 1949. Plumtree station closed to passengers in February 1949 and to goods in 1965. Only the Leicestershire village station of Old Dalby remained open as a stop for local trains (diesel units replaced steam in 1958).

The line, however, was still a major route for expresses. On 1st June 1880 the Midland Railway had started running Leeds to London St Pancras expresses using this route, and for a further 80 years, whatever the problems of the local services, the expresses continued to thunder along the line.

But then came the Beeching report, which pointed out that the duplication of routes was wasteful. As we have mentioned, there were three routes between Nottingham and London, the Great Central line, the Midland line via Trent Junction, and the Midland line via Melton. Two of them needed to be closed, and the choice fell on the Great Central and on the line via Melton. The Nottingham–Melton service on this line, still calling at Old Dalby, would also be withdrawn.

The local service went first, the last train running on 16th April 1966, but at that time British Rail seemed in no hurry to implement the Beeching recommendation to end the Nottingham to London express service. However, services were gradually re-routed via Trent Junction until only one express a day in each direction was running via Melton. Then in May 1966 British Rail showed its hand and announced its proposal to discontinue all passenger services on the line. The last timetabled passenger train was the London to Sheffield express, leaving St Pancras at 5.55 pm, on Saturday, 29th April 1967. Freight traffic continued

The bridge over the River Trent at Colwick. The Cotgrave Colliery line viaduct is seen at the right-hand side of the picture. This could provide a solution for crossing the river if the Nottingham–Melton line was ever restored as a through route. (Rodger Smith)

An intact bridge from the old Melton line carrying the trackbed, now used as a footpath and cycleway, over the road. The two cyclists have just come down from the track. The bridge is high enough to allow room for the double decker buses of the old West Bridgford transport authority. (Rodger Smith)

to use the line, but maintenance was reduced, and speed restrictions were introduced.

In 1968 the Queen made her first visit to Nottingham for 13 years, and the Royal Train used the line, so that the last known non-freight train to travel between Melton and Nottingham was the most prestigious train of all.

Freight traffic itself ceased in October 1968. The part of the line south of Nottingham Midland station was closed on 4th November 1968. The actual railway was then severed and the rails taken up at the Nottingham end, between London Road junction and Edwalton. No longer would passengers in a train held up by signals be able to watch the cricket at the Trent Bridge ground! Though this, it seems, was little more than one of those cherished myths – part of the ground could be glimpsed, but not enough to give a clear impression of the play.

The short section north of the River Trent, from the London Road junction, has now been built over with industrial buildings. Though only three miles of the actual railway are missing, the conversion of the Lady Bay bridge to road traffic effectively blocks the route. But there is a campaign to restore the line. Because Lady Bay bridge is an integral part of Nottingham's road network, an alternative is needed. Campaigners have pointed out that a short new stretch of line of about three miles in length could connect Plumtree to the Cotgrave Colliery line (still in place though not in use) from where a viaduct leads to the Colwick bridge over the Trent.

South of the river, through the Nottingham suburb of West Bridgford, from a point just south of the A6520 main road (Ordnance Survey grid reference: SK 586383), some two miles of the former trackbed are intact and run on a high embankment and then into a cutting. This section has been turned into an attractive footpath and cycleway.

The footpath ends at Boundary Road, West Bridgford (SK 589358) but the route, where the cutting has been filled in, can still be traced over rough ground for a further quarter of a mile, as far as the bridge taking the Lodge Farm access road over it. South of here new houses and gardens have obscured the route. Edwalton station has been completely demolished and the site developed.

A final piece of accessible trackbed can be reached by a footpath from the A606 (SK 593348). The place marked on the map as Hill Farm is now a small group of residences converted from the farm buildings. The path goes through them before turning sharp left and curving round to a bridge over the trackbed, here densely overgrown, as the picture shows.

South of the Hill Farm complex the route runs mainly through open countryside, until it reaches the county boundary with Leicestershire. Here rails still exist, for this is Railtrack's test track, which has been used for testing the Advanced Passenger Train (the 'tilting train'), the High Speed Freight Vehicle and the Pendolino train. The original attraction of the line for testing was its proximity to British Rail's research laboratories in Derby.

The Hill Farm footpath leads to a bridge over the trackbed, which at this point is densely overgrown. (Rodger Smith)

The old Plumtree station lay between Plumtree and Keyworth, the latter now a much bigger place than its neighbour. During the Second World War the bodies of two Polish airmen who had been killed in a crash during a training flight from nearby Tollerton airfield were brought to Plumtree station, which was used as a temporary mortuary. In 1945 German prisoners of war who had been kept at Tollerton Hall were taken to Plumtree station on their way to being repatriated.

Efforts to convince his railway superiors that there was potential for rail traffic from Plumtree and Edwalton were made in the 1950s by John Ingamells, joint stationmaster for the two stations, which were then used only as goods depots. He managed to get occasional holiday and football excursion trains to stop. The last passenger train to visit Edwalton seems to have

The old trackbed runs into a cutting. The steps on the left of the picture are the access from Boundary Road, West Bridgford. (Rodger Smith)

been a football excursion on Saturday, 15th November 1958, and Plumtree saw holiday excursions to Mablethorpe and Skegness in the summer of 1959. In 1982 the Plumtree station buildings became a restaurant specialising in French cuisine.

South of Plumtree there are very few places where the line can be seen either from the road or from footpaths.

Widmerpool station was closed to regular passenger traffic in 1949, the only protest, it appears, coming from a Mr Brown, who had been catching the train to Nottingham every weekday from Widmerpool for 30 years. The last train from Nottingham to Widmerpool ran on 26th February 1949. The station remained open for goods and parcels until 1965, when it was finally closed. Its fate was to be the same as that of Plumtree station, being turned into a restaurant (the Pullman) though it was more extensively altered for its new role.

Just after the site of Upper Broughton station the line leaves

Nottinghamshire and enters Leicestershire (curiously the two adjacent villages of Upper Broughton and Nether Broughton are in different counties). The stationmaster's house at Upper Broughton is now a private residence.

3

Relics Of The Great Northern Railway

London Road Low Level and High Level Stations

An architectural masterpiece – T.C. Hine's Nottingham London Road station built for the Great Northern Railway, which had its greatest days as a terminus in the 19th century. By the time this picture was taken in the 1920s it was under-used, after much of its traffic had been transferred to Nottingham Victoria. (Stations UK, Southport)

The commanding officer had given his orders. His troops were in position. The enemy was on its way, unaware of the trap that had been prepared. The date was 2nd August 1852.

The 'commanding officer' was Mr Pettifer, and he was the stationmaster at Nottingham. Like his 'troops', he was an employee of the Midland Railway, and while he was almost

55

certainly acting with the blessing of Midland Railway head-quarters at Derby, perhaps even of the directors themselves, on the spot it was Mr Pettifer who co-ordinated all the operations.

The 'enemy' was the Grantham to Nottingham train run by a small railway company, which went by the cumbersome name of the Ambergate, Nottingham, Boston & Eastern Junction Railway (ANB&EJR). The train steamed into Nottingham station over the Midland lines, as it believed it was legally entitled to do.

After the ANB&EJR train had pulled up in the station and discharged its passengers, its crew detached the locomotive (which had been hired from the Great Northern Railway) prior to turning it round and steaming to the other end of the train in order to re-connect it and make the return journey to Grantham. But then Mr Pettifer ordered the first of his forces into action. As the ANB&EJR engine started its manoeuvring, it suddenly found that there was a Midland locomotive in front blocking its way forward. Then another Midland locomotive came up behind so that it was effectively captured. There were no doubt vehement arguments and loud protests, and the driver of the ANB&EJR locomotive was said to have made a desperate effort to charge the engine in front, but to no avail. The Midland Railway captors had their orders. The ANB&EJR engine was taken off by them into an old engine house.

Then Mr Pettifer ordered his second line of troops into action. No sooner was the 'enemy' engine safely in the shed than a gang of platelayers started work outside. Normally their work involved laying railway lines, but on this occasion they took them up, just to make sure that the ANB&EJR engine was well and truly marooned.

This high-handed action demonstrates just how fiercely the Midland Railway was prepared to defend its then virtual monopoly in Nottinghamshire. At one time it had harboured its own ambitions to take over the ANB&EJR, but had been frustrated by a Great Northern shareholder, Graham Hutchinson, who had bought many of the ANB&EJR shares.

The Midland's monopoly was disliked by the Nottingham Corporation and by Parliament. Undeterred, however, the Midland Railway continued to fight fiercely in Parliament and the courts to keep its most dangerous rival, the Great Northern

56

Railway, out of Nottinghamshire. To the east the Great Northern was completing a direct line from York via Grantham to London, running into King's Cross station, which would be one of the most attractive routes in the country.

Nottingham Corporation had given its support to the ANB&EJR when it constructed its independent line from a junction with the Great Northern line at Grantham to a junction with the Midland's Nottingham to Lincoln line at Colwick, on the east side of Nottingham. And authority had then imposed on the Midland Railway the right of the ANB&EJR to run its trains over the last stretch of Midland tracks and into Nottingham station.

But the Midland had driven a hard bargain in exchange for this, insisting on crippling contributions from the ANB&EJR, while the Midland's manoeuvres in Parliament forced the ANB&EJR to buy out, at great expense, the Nottingham and Grantham canals before they were allowed to proceed. But the Midland Railway's harsh treatment of the smaller company was about to boomerang. Although the ANB&EJR had started running trains on its Grantham and Nottingham service in 1850, because of its over-extended financial position it was soon in difficulty. In 1852 it had to surrender its independence and enter into a 'working agreement' with the Great Northern.

The Great Northern then took over the running of the ANB&EJR, and advertised that the Great Northern would now be running 'through coaches' from London to Nottingham. For the Midland Railway the words 'Great Northern' were a red rag to a bull. So the Midland wielded its formidable legal resources to get an injunction preventing the through train concept, but the GNR went ahead anyway. And it was the first train to include such a through coach that Mr Pettifer and his army so effectively ambushed.

After the battle of Nottingham station the conflict moved back to the courts, and eventually, seven months later, the captive engine was released. The Great Northern's acquisition of the ANB&EJR had to be recognised, but the rivalry between the two companies continued. The Midland Railway started refusing to convey all ANB&EJR 'through' traffic from Nottingham station, so that the ANB&EJR had to carry goods by horse-drawn road

Still looking good. This view shows the best of the T.C. Hine design with the porte cochère still standing proudly out from the front of the building. (Rodger Smith)

transport to Colwick, which was the terminus of its own independent line. This ANB&EJR line ran between Colwick, then a tiny village in the country three miles east of Nottingham, to Grantham, where it linked up with the Great Northern system.

Parliamentary Acts of 1853 and 1854 enabled the Great Northern to take over the assets of the ANB&EJR. Now more than ever determined to run trains into Nottingham, the Great Northern decided the only solution was to build its own Nottingham terminus. It therefore got permission to run its own tracks, so no longer was there that risky business of having running rights over Midland lines. These tracks ran from Netherfield, near Colwick, to a new Nottingham terminus on London Road, Nottingham, at what was called East Croft. The original junction with the Midland line at Colwick was removed, and it was not until nearly a century later, under British

The magnificent train shed at London Road Low Level station has been glassed in and sensitively converted into a sports hall. (Rodger Smith)

Railways, that it was restored so that Grantham trains could run once again into Nottingham Midland station.

The handsome new Great Northern station, then as now recognised as an architectural gem, was designed by a leading Nottingham architect, Thomas Chambers Hine, and built at a cost of £20,000. Hine worked on many buildings in Nottingham, including the remodelling of Nottingham Castle.

Nottingham London Road station opened, together with the new three miles of line (including a bridge over the Nottingham Canal), on 3rd October 1857. It was used for all Great Northern traffic into Nottingham until the opening of the Victoria station in 1900, when all Great Northern passenger trains were transferred there, and then until 1944, for trains between Nottingham and Northampton (a service operated by the London & North Western Railway). After 12th May 1944, they too transferred to Nottingham Victoria.

Nottingham's London Road High Level station, with the sign 'Alight here for Trent Bridge cricket and football grounds'. (Stations UK, Southport)

Subsequently the station was closed to the general public but continued to be used for merchandise and parcels traffic for the LNER lines running into Nottingham, and in 1967 it was refurbished as Nottingham Parcel Concentration Depot. Later the premises were sold off. The station buildings were faithfully restored, with great attention to detail, although they are now used as offices and a health centre, and are not open to the general public. The trainshed has been glazed and turned into a sports hall. The official address of the premises is still Low Level Station, The Great Northern Close, London Road, Nottingham.

The station building is in bright red brick with richly carved stone dressings, with ornamental iron cresting and elegant chimneys at the top. There were balustrades and cornices, and rich ornamentation. According to the 'Bible' of station architecture, Gordon Biddle's *Britain's Historic Railway Buildings*, 'the station most closely resembles a French chateau with Jacobean additions'.

The main building is in two storeys, with the lower storey in its railway operation days containing the booking hall, waiting rooms and stationmaster's office, and the upper storey containing

A side view, taken in 1947, of Nottingham London Road High Level station. Part of the ground-floor entrance, which can be seen behind the rag-and-bone men with their handcart, is now a restaurant. (Stations UK, Southport)

Great Northern administrative offices. A major feature, which can still be appreciated from the outside, is the large carriage portico (*porte cochère* in architectural terms) on iron columns painted to resemble stone. The platforms were covered by an iron roof and were approached by a large doorway in the main buildings.

When Nottingham Victoria station was opened, the regular service of trains between Grantham and Nottingham were re-routed via a new spur from Weekday Cross junction to Trent Lane junction and called at the new station of London Road High Level. This may have been in an unattractive part of the town of Nottingham, surrounded by industrial premises, but it was an astonishing piece of civil engineering. A viaduct, which carried some of the Great Northern lines into the new Victoria station, was constructed, a massive latticework girder structure over gasworks sidings and two canals. The station itself was an island platform on top of the viaduct, accessed by a staircase from street level. Also at street level were the subway and booking hall in

61

The last remaining piece of viaduct from Nottingham's London Road High Level station. (Rodger Smith)

red brick. On the platforms above, the buildings were mostly in wood, with well-designed panelling and a gable glass roof and canopy supported on cast-iron columns. A feature many people remember is the large board advising passengers to 'alight here' for the Trent Bridge cricket and football grounds. The football grounds are those of Nottingham Forest and Notts County, and the Trent Bridge cricket ground is not only the home of the Nottinghamshire county side but also, of course, one of England's traditional Test Match venues.

The High Level station was finally closed in 1967 after the Grantham line trains were diverted into Nottingham Midland station. Today all that can be seen is a truncated piece of viaduct, best viewed from the Nottingham Canal, which flows parallel with London Road.

Another station that claimed to serve Trent Bridge cricket ground and both Notts County and Nottingham Forest football grounds was Arkwright Street, a nondescript inner city station a

Arkwright Street station pictured in the 1930s. (Stations UK, Southport)

little to the south of the High Level and Low Level stations. Arkwright Street station closed in 1963, but, as we saw in Chapter 1, was temporarily re-opened in 1967 to take the last remaining traffic from Nottingham Victoria after the closure of that station. Arkwright Street then had a further 20 months of life before it closed definitely, and fell victim to the demolition hammer.

4
Where Housing Estates Now Stand

The Back Line into Derbyshire

A coal train passes through Basford & Bulwell station, 1947. (H.C. Casserley, Berkhamsted)

'Keep crossing clear'. Travelling along Victoria Road in the Nottingham suburb of Netherfield, the cautious motorist sees in front of him modern warning lights and signs, informing him that a railway level crossing lies ahead. He will keep a careful look-out in case the lights start flashing and the gates begin to close.

But in fact these lights never flash, and the crossing gates have not closed for some years. On each side of the road the railway

Modern warning lights and signs are in place to inform motorists that they are approaching a level crossing at Victoria Road, Netherfield, Nottingham ...

but the crossing gates are bolted shut ...

and it does not look as if the line has been much used recently. (Author)

65

lines are still there, but weeds are growing between the tracks. For this is another of Nottinghamshire's lost railways.

The railway was officially called the Derbyshire and Staffordshire Extension, but was more familiarly known as the Back Line, because instead of taking the direct route from Nottingham to Derby it went in a large semi-circle north of the city.

This was yet another ambitious attempt by the Great Northern Railway company to invade what had always been regarded as Midland Railway territory. On 25th July 1872 the Great Northern saw its Derbyshire and Staffordshire Act passed through Parliament. The Midland Railway already had the direct route between Nottingham and Derby. At first glance the route being proposed by the Great Northern seemed a long way round, but it was deliberately planned, to come close to every major coalmine in the Erewash Valley coalfield, even though these mines were already being served by the Midland Railway.

Derby lies to the west of Nottingham, but the line started to the east, at a junction with the Great Northern's Nottingham to Grantham line. It then curved north. From the junction a short section is still intact (it is this section which crosses Victoria Road, Netherfield, by the level crossing). The continued existence of this part of the line is because it was used for a time for access to Gedling Colliery, and then it was thought it might one day be incorporated into the Nottingham tram network.

The route continued through Daybrook, Bulwell and Kimberley (whose population of 4,000 had asked the company to provide an access for them to the railway system). It reached Awsworth (with a branch to Pinxton) in 1875 and thence from a junction at Awsworth penetrated to Ilkeston and Derby (the very town where the Great Northern's arch-rival, the Midland Railway, had its headquarters) and Egginton Junction in 1878. From Egginton, with running powers over the North Staffordshire Railway, the GNR reached Burton upon Trent in 1881 (where it could gain access to the brewery trade) and later Stafford, a total of 40½ miles.

The Derbyshire Extension proved to be a difficult line to construct, because it lay against the grain of the land, and had to cross both hills and valleys, making the problem of keeping a level gradient unusually difficult. Trains came out of

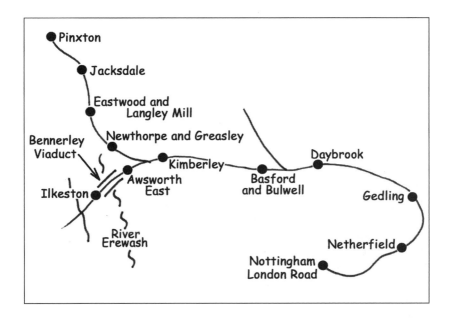

Nottingham's London Road terminus in an easterly direction, then, after 3½ miles, at Netherfield Junction, they curved back to the north-west, in a semi-circle climbing past Gedling station and then, even more steeply, to Mapperley tunnel. From there they travelled downhill to Daybrook (where modern housing has obliterated almost every trace of the track), and on to Basford & Bulwell station.

Basford & Bulwell station (originally New Basford, but changed to Basford & Bulwell after a few months, and finally renamed Basford North in 1953), opened in 1876, was intended to serve a major catchment area of the north Nottingham suburbs so was built on substantial lines, with an iron footbridge connecting the two platforms. It had its own goods yard and sidings with a goods shed, cattle dock and coal store, so that there were nine pairs of lines at this one site. It has been calculated that in 1900 as many as 216 (sometimes more) freight and passenger trains went through each day.

The importance of the station, and of the line, was reduced in 1923 when the Grouping brought together the Great Central and

Children and parents from Gedling All Hallows Parish Church Sunday School waiting on Gedling station for their special seaside excursion to Skegness, 1954. Note the small boy who is bending forwards to see if he can spot the train coming. (Mrs Nancy Moulds)

the Great Northern into one company, the LNER, since the Great Central gave a more direct route into the centre of Nottingham.

New housing has now completely covered the site of Basford & Bulwell station. It stood roughly at the western end of Saxondale Drive, which itself is approximately on the alignment of a later LNER line joining the Great Northern to the Great Central. A nearby cul-de-sac, off Highbury Road, is called Northern Court, the last reminder of the bustling railway activity that was going on here 100 years ago.

Westwards from Basford & Bulwell the line crossed the

Midland Railway's Nottingham to Mansfield line at a height of 40 feet by an iron lattice deck span, and then there was the viaduct of nine brick arches carrying it 50 feet above the River Leen (demolished, and adjoining embankments flattened, in the 1970s; the site is today Garton Close).

Towards Kimberley there was a cutting, 55 feet deep, and 2½ miles long, made through magnesian limestone, which was difficult to work, with a short tunnel at Watnall. Kimberley station, at the end of the cutting, had buildings of red brick. At one time it displayed a large board stating 'Kimberley for Watnall, Nuthall and Giltbrook', On the up platform there was a waiting room, and in addition, until the 1930s, on the up platform, a wooden shed for the use of miners.

A little further towards Ilkeston there was Awsworth station (opened on 1st November 1880) and the line crossed the Erewash Valley (and the county boundary) by the Bennerley viaduct (erected July 1876 to November 1877 and operational until 1968), one of the wonders of the district, engineered by Richard Johnson, a huge steel trestle of 16 spans, 60 feet high above the River Erewash. Its lattice girders are supported on piers of ten tubular columns, arranged 2-3-3-2, the outermost pairs being at a slightly diagonal angle. The columns are set on bases of blue bricks capped by stone. It is one of only two (out of five) wrought iron trestle viaducts that still exist in Britain (the other being at Meldon in South Devon), the trestle system of crossing gorges or deep valleys being more usually associated with the USA. The use of wrought iron was dictated by the nature of the ground, which was not firm enough to support a brick structure, except at its western continuation, which took the Great Northern line over the Midland Railway's Erewash Valley line. The ironwork had been prefabricated, and was assembled on site.

The Bennerley viaduct (SK 474439) is a listed building, but removal of the embankments at either end have marooned it. Even today, in its isolation, it remains an impressive sight, a full quarter of a mile long and 56 feet high. It is regrettable that such a magnificent structure remains unused, but when funds become available there are plans to make it part of a cycleway.

Beyond the viaduct the line passed into Derbyshire, and so strictly speaking out of the remit of this book. We might just

The Bennerley viaduct, a Grade II listed structure, going from nowhere to nowhere but still majestically striding across the Erewash Valley. (Judy Kingscott)

mention that for its invasion of the Midland Railway stronghold of Derby the Great Northern built a new station, Derby Friargate. Their handsome bridge for this line still dominates Friargate, one of Derby's main thoroughfares.

Stations between Gedling and Egginton Junction (the latter being with the North Staffordshire Railway) were mostly constructed to a standard design, based on a single-storey block with a station house attached, and a timber waiting room on the opposite platform. However, Basford & Bulwell station was in white limestone and darker stone giving a checkerboard effect.

Before 1939 there were nine passenger trains a day on this line in each direction between Nottingham Victoria and Basford. Earlier, up to 1934, there had also been two trains in each direction taking miners to and from Gedling Colliery, using

Basford North station, 1955. Locomotive 64235 with the Nottingham to Pinxton stopping train. Note the decorative effect on the chimneys. (R.M. Casserley, Berkhamsted)

ancient coaches with wooden seats. Between the two world wars this route lost traffic heavily to buses.

After the Second World War the daily weekday service was reduced to five trains each way, though the line was also heavily used by coal and freight traffic, and also by trains taking iron ore to Stanton Ironworks. During the summer months there were also excursion trains picking up from the smaller stations and avoiding the diversion into Nottingham Victoria. These were very popular and on a fine Sunday as many as eight trains would run to the coast. In addition there was a regular Saturday train, Birmingham New Street to Skegness, which also picked up on this line.

There were a number of branches from this line, not counting those serving collieries, all now closed and 'lost railways'. One (opened in 1882) was from the Leen Valley Junction through Hucknall to Annesley, where the line joined the Great Central, and along which there were stopping trains to Nottingham. Another branch went from Ilkeston northwards to Heanor

71

Newthorpe & Greasley branch-line station, pictured in 1950, one of a number demolished to make way for the A610 road. (H.C. Casserley, Berkhamsted)

(1881), and was served by a local service, and southwards to Stanton Ironworks, and another from Awsworth Junction to Pinxton.

The Awsworth to Pinxton branch line had five passenger stations. Close to Awsworth was the Giltbrook viaduct (built 1873–1875), known as '40 bridges', over the Giltbrook valley. It was in a gentle S curve shape. It was scheduled for preservation after the Pinxton branch had been closed in 1964, but its site was required for the building of the new A610 bypass road. It was therefore demolished in the spring and summer of 1973, and the rubble from the viaduct was used as hardcore filling for the road construction.

The first station on the branch, Newthorpe & Greasley for Shipley Gate, was closed to passenger traffic on 7th January 1963 and to goods traffic on 16th May 1966. The buildings and bridges were also demolished in 1973 during the construction of the bypass.

One of the stations on this branch was at Eastwood & Langley

Mill. Eastwood is the home town of the novelist D.H. Lawrence, and in his best-known and largely autobiographical novel *Sons and Lovers*, the hero, Paul Morel, catches the train at 'Bestwood' to go to Nottingham. But there is no clue in the narrative as to whether he travelled on the Great Northern line, or left from the Eastwood Midland station a few hundred yards away. The A610 now runs over the site, and there is no trace of railway or station.

The station at Jacksdale was subject to many name changes. When it opened to passengers in 1876 it was called Codnor Park & Selston, but in 1901 this was simplified to Codnor Park. Later it was Codnor Park for Ironville & Jacksdale, then finally (in 1950) Jacksdale, to distinguish it from the Codnor Park station of the old Midland Railway. The station was actually on a brick viaduct, and passengers had to climb a staircase to the platforms, the booking and parcels office being at street level. Here again bridges and station buildings were comprehensively demolished. Pye Hill station came next, but opencast coalmining has removed most traces of the line, apart from some trackbed north of the B600 road. Here the Great Northern line was running almost

Jacksdale station pictured in 1963, towards the end of its working life. (Stations UK, Southport)

73

exactly parallel with the Midland Railway's line, the two being never more than a few hundred yards apart. Pinxton (for South Normanton) was the terminus station of this branch, and had a wooden waiting shed for coalminers, who often used 'Paddy' trains, which did not appear in the advertised timetables (see Chapter 8).

Passenger services between Nottingham and Pinxton started in 1876, with nine trains each way on weekdays, the journey taking one hour, but the number of trains was later reduced. The passenger service continued until 9th September 1962, running parallel, as we saw in the case of Eastwood, with the Midland Railway's Erewash Valley line. It is the latter which is still carrying traffic today (mainly goods traffic, as many of its stations have closed). The Great Northern's Pinxton branch has almost entirely been obliterated.

Later, with the Nottingham Suburban Railway (see Chapter 6), it was possible to run a circuit Basford–Daybrook–Gedling–London Road High Level–Victoria–Basford, 10 miles long and taking about 40 minutes. In its heyday between the two world wars passenger trains on the line ran from Stafford, Burton upon Trent or Derby to Nottingham and Grantham, and to seaside holiday resorts. After the Second World War the services were simplified to a regular run between Nottingham Victoria and Derby Friargate stations.

A major setback for the Back Line came on 23rd January 1925, when a length of roof collapsed in the Mapperley tunnel, always a problem location because of subsidence from the workings of Gedling Colliery. Then in the late 1950s the line was affected by colliery subsidence, and speed limits were imposed. It was finally announced that the tunnel would be closed on 4th April 1960 and all traffic diverted to other routes. The last ordinary passenger train left Nottingham Victoria for Basford at 6.10 pm on 4th April. A bus service was substituted, calling at the various stations, with rail tickets being issued at the station booking office, and this lasted until 2nd April 1962.

Services at Kimberley station (there was also a Midland station at Kimberley until 1917) lasted until September 1964. The last stationmaster was G. Frank Pike, whose father, George Charles Pike, had earlier been stationmaster there from 1912 to 1932.

74

Demolition in the late 1960s of a former Great Northern bridge at Basford, part of the comprehensive dismantling of the Derbyshire Extension line. (Courtesy of Nottingham City Council Leisure and Community Services Central Library Local Studies Library)

Confirmation of the withdrawal of the Nottingham Victoria to Derby Friargate service, which had been prescribed in the Beeching report, was announced in June 1964, and the last train left Victoria for Derby at 10.30 pm on Saturday, 5th September 1964. The service of course to some extent duplicated the one from Nottingham Midland station to Derby Midland on the more direct route. On 6th March 1966 workmen started taking up the tracks along most of the length of the line, and much of its course has now been built on.

5
A Fallen Colossus

The Colwick Yards, Sheds and Depots

Even an aerial picture can only give a partial glimpse of the immensity of Colwick Yard. The earliest buildings, dating from 1876, are on the right, and these were steadily added to. The structures include locomotive depots and repair shops, as well as offices and canteens. (Courtesy of Nottingham City Council Leisure and Community Services Central Library Local Studies Library)

Two hundred years ago Colwick, four miles east of Nottingham city centre, was a sleepy, insignificant hamlet. One hundred years ago it was a railway town, with the extensive marshalling yards, engine sheds and depots in operation 24 hours a day,

The original nameplate still survives on the bridge over the River Trent erected on behalf of the Ambergate, Nottingham, Boston & Eastern Junction Railway. (Rodger Smith)

365 days a year, with perhaps 200 steam locomotives there at any one time. It was a colossus of the railway system.

Today it's all quiet again. The yards, sheds, depots and locomotives, the boilermakers, welders, loaders and shunters, the steam whistles and the clanging wagons – they have all gone. A sprawling industrial estate occupies the site, and not much seems to happen.

Colwick did make an early appearance on the railway map. When the Ambergate, Nottingham, Boston & Eastern Junction Railway, which we met in Chapter 3, laid its line from Grantham towards Nottingham, it joined the Midland Railway's Nottingham to Lincoln route at Colwick. Then the hamlet's railway importance increased immeasurably when it was here that the Great Northern's Derbyshire Extension, described in the last chapter, left the Great Northern's Nottingham to Grantham line to start its long curve westwards.

A principal Great Northern motive in building the Derbyshire Extension had been to serve as many coalmines as possible, and this meant that somewhere there had to be considerable coal-handling facilities. Coal trains needed to be made up in marshalling yards, requiring multiple-line operation and crews experienced in shunting operations. London was the big market for coal, but there was also considerable custom from East Anglia. Somewhere was needed, too, for more and more engine sheds. What Colwick offered, as well as its strategic junction location, was a large area of flat land between the railway and the River Trent. Much of Nottingham itself is hilly, so this was probably the closest to the city where such land was available.

As time went on and the Great Northern extended its operations, more and more engine sheds were constructed, and there also grew up a miscellany of buildings to house the various operations necessary to running a major railway enterprise – repair shops, stores, canteens, and offices. When the Saxondale Junction to Melton Mowbray line (which we shall meet in Chapter 10) was opened in 1879, it was operated jointly by the Great Northern and the London & North Western Railway (LNWR). The latter was at the same time granted running rights over the Derbyshire Extension, and so needed its own facilities. An engine shed and sidings devoted to the LNWR was therefore added to the Colwick complex. Then the opening of the Great Northern's Leen Valley line in 1881 brought more collieries into the GNR network, particularly the highly productive new pits at Newstead and Annesley, and further development was required at Colwick, including lodging accommodation for train crews. At their peak the yards were a maelstrom of activity. The overall supervision of the site was entrusted to an official called the Yardmaster, and he was given his own substantial residence, Ambergate House.

An extensive modernisation was carried out at Colwick in 1936, including the building of a huge plant for the automatic coal-loading of locomotives. A landmark for miles around, this was often known, from its angular shape, as 'the Cenotaph'.

In the 1960s, however, the activity was becoming noticeably reduced. British industry no longer relied so exclusively on coal, and the phasing out of steam locomotives made the Cenotaph

78

redundant. It was demolished at the end of 1971. Also, with the closure of many of the former Great Northern lines, there was no need for the same number of locomotives to be kept.

Colwick depot was closed to steam locomotives in 1966 (by 1968 steam had been phased out altogether from the regular railway network). In October 1969 an observer noted some diesel locomotives there, but the place was clearly in decline.

For marshalling yards as for passenger lines and stations, rationalisation was now the order of the day. And Colwick had a major rival. The Toton marshalling yards, first created by the Midland Railway, located on the south-western boundary of Nottinghamshire, had also benefited from the importance of coal in Nottinghamshire, and had grown until they could boast of being the largest marshalling yards in Europe.

Finally Colwick was serving only traffic from the Gedling and

Rectory Junction, controlling the entrance to Colwick Yard, was just to the right of this picture. Sometimes the congestion in the yard was so great that shunting took place as far back as the bridge. (Rodger Smith)

Cotgrave collieries plus trip working to Toton. The yard was completely closed on 12th April 1970.

Rectory Junction, close to the bridge that still carries the main Nottingham–Grantham line over the River Trent, housed a large signal box controlling many of the movements from that line into and out of Colwick. The signal box also controlled the movement of coal trains on the branch to Cotgrave Colliery. This branch line is still in place, but is not at present used for traffic.

The two-track oil terminal next to Rectory Junction on the Nottingham–Grantham line is the only remnant of Colwick Yard, a tiny fraction of what was once one of the country's major centres of railway activity.

6
Built For Early Commuters

The Nottingham Suburban Railway

The locomotive on the last train to pass over the Nottingham Suburban Railway, 1951, running round before being re-coupled to take the excursion train on the return journey. The Cooper's Arms on Porchester Road is still there and can help locate the site of the former station. (Henry Priestley, by courtesy of Nottingham City Council Leisure and Community Services Central Library Local Studies Library)

Suburban. These days the word has connotations of something dull and boring. But to a group of 19th century Nottingham businessmen suburbs were new and exciting, and rich in commercial opportunities. Which is why they came to build the Nottingham Suburban Railway.

By the 1880s the city of Nottingham had expanded into the surrounding villages and hamlets. Those villages and hamlets had joined up and become suburbs. And the residents of those new suburbs needed transport. Up until nearly the end of the 19th century the only competitor to the railways for land-based public transport in towns was the service offered by horse-drawn trams and omnibuses. These were obviously slow, could carry only light loads, and could not travel long distances. Consequently they were never seen in the suburbs.

In London and in other big cities the Underground railway and what we would now call commuter lines were enjoying great success. So some Nottingham businessmen decided to create such a line on their own patch. They came to an agreement with the Great Northern Railway for that company to work the line, but the Nottingham Suburban Railway actually remained a separate legal entity until the 1923 Grouping, when it was incorporated into the LNER.

There was already in Nottingham an outer ring railway, in the form of the Derbyshire Extension described in Chapter 4, but that line had been laid out primarily to link up coalmines, with passenger traffic a secondary consideration. The Nottingham Suburban Railway, so its backers thought, could be designed to complement the Derbyshire Extension and connect up with it, as well as providing a more direct route into the city.

However, passengers were not the only motive for the railway. One of its leading promoters was Nottingham businessman Robert Mellors, who was chairman of the Nottingham Patent Brick Company. It just so happened that that company's brickworks at Thorneywood and Mapperley would be served by the proposed line, in fact by its only branch, a short run of nine chains (198 yards) in length, over half of it being in tunnel.

Another director of the brick company was the surveyor Edward Parry, and it was natural that he should be selected as the engineer and surveyor for the new line. The bill placed before Parliament was strongly supported by the Nottingham Corporation.

By October 1886 the route had been staked out. Work started

The block of flats built on the site of Thorneywood station on the Nottingham Suburban Railway was named after the line's chief engineer, Edward Parry, following a suggestion made by Sneinton historian Stephen Best, here pictured at the entrance to the development.

in June 1888. The line, 3¾ miles long, ran from a junction with the Great Northern at Trent Lane, Sneinton, then directly north to a junction with the Great Northern's Derbyshire Extension at Daybrook, with stations at Thorneywood, St Ann's Well and Sherwood. This cut out the long curve of the Derbyshire Extension.

Because of the hilly nature of the city, the Nottingham Suburban Railway proved an expensive line to build, with four tunnels totalling 1,103 yards. This meant that one-sixth of the whole route was in tunnels. There were also seven brick arched bridges, nine girder bridges, of which three were over 100 feet in span, eight culverts, retaining walls of considerable size, embankments and deep cuttings. The line was formally opened on 2nd December 1889.

Inbound trains ran from Daybrook, via the three intermediate

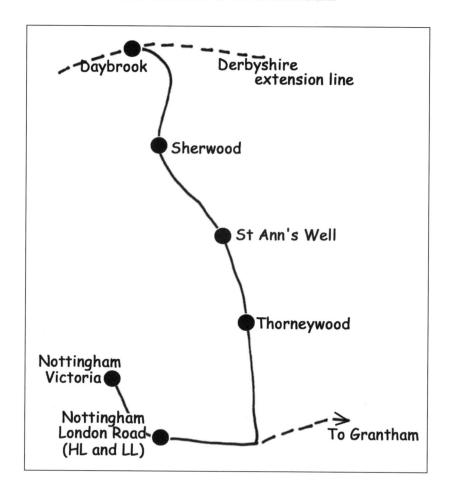

stations, and then into the Great Northern's terminus at Nottingham London Road station. Each of the three stations lay in its own valley, and the platforms were generous in size, in preparation for the anticipated large-scale commuter traffic, which unfortunately never did develop. Sherwood station, for example, had a substantial brick-built booking hall, brick-built waiting rooms on both platforms, and extensive wooden canopies, again over both platforms. It has now completely disappeared, though the new road created to access the station

Although not definitively identified, this picture of a contractor with his men and a railway engine is thought to have been taken during the construction of the Nottingham Suburban Railway. (Courtesy of Nottingham City Council Leisure and Community Services Central Library Local Studies Library)

(an extension to the existing Winchester Street plus the road now called Mapperley Rise) still exists. The station was built on a curve, with the two platforms connected by a wrought iron lattice footbridge. The site is now occupied by two tower blocks of flats and rows of lock-up garages, which follow the curve of the original trackbed.

St Ann's Well station also had sidings, and a goods shed as well. Here, however, the up platform was all-wood construction, giving a temporary feel. The station was close to where the

85

Sherwood station, pictured in around 1900. (Courtesy of Nottingham City Council Leisure and Community Services Central Library Local Studies Library)

railway crossed Wells Road at an angle by a bridge which has now disappeared. The two platforms were, as at Sherwood, linked by a wrought iron lattice footbridge. Most of the station area is now the site of modern flats, but the station house is still there, converted into a private residence.

Thorneywood station (SK 591409) was built where the line emerged from one of the tunnels on the line. Thorneywood also had sidings used for domestic coal traffic, and the short branch to the brickworks. West of the railway at Thorneywood a new road, Marmion Road, which is still there, had to be created, and two streets, Holly Gardens and Thorneywood Rise, had to be truncated to make room for the station.

The running of the entire railway – including staffing, locomotives and rolling stock – was entrusted to the Great Northern Railway (which could then retain 55 per cent of the gross receipts). The first train, on 2nd December 1889, carried a party of railway dignitaries and a number of ordinary passengers. The journey was not without incident. There had

St Ann's Well station in its heyday before the First World War. (John Marshall, by courtesy of Nottingham City Council Leisure and Community Services Central Library Local Studies Library)

been a complex last-minute dispute between the contractor for the line, J.P. Edwards, and the railway company, in which the former claimed that the contract was not completed and he still had possession of the line. The train duly left Nottingham London Road station, but when it started to move from the main Great Northern line on to newly-built line at Trent Lane junction an agent of the contractor stopped the train with a red flag. There was an altercation, but the Great Northern's locomotive superintendent Mr Cockspur, who was with the driver on the footplate, announced that they were going to continue. The contractor's agent, a Mr Colson, then stepped aside but placed his red flag on the rail, so that the train had to run over it. On the return journey from Daybrook a ticket inspection was carried out at Thorneywood station, and the

87

Most of the site of St Ann's Well station has been built over, but the station house survives as a private residence

contractor Mr Edwards and his assistant J. Scott, who were on the train, were reported for failing to have tickets.

Nothing significant came of this argument, and by January 1890 there were ten trains running out from Nottingham London Road station along the line, and nine in the opposite direction. Some of the trains continued to Newstead on the Great Northern's Leen Valley line. By 1895 there was also a through train to Ilkeston, and on Fridays this was extended to Derby Friargate.

Unfortunately within the short space of 12 years two developments were about to make the Nottingham Suburban Railway superfluous. One was the Great Central Railway (see Chapter 1), which in 1900 opened up an even more direct route into Nottingham city centre, and the other was the introduction into Nottingham in 1901 of electric trams. The very first tram route opened on 1st January 1901, running along Mansfield Road (then, as now, one of Nottingham's major thoroughfares) as far as Winchester Street, close to Sherwood station. Trams reached Thorneywood at the end of 1910 and by 1915 had got to Arnold and Daybrook.

The number of trains stopping at stations on the Nottingham Suburban line was gradually reduced. In order to achieve faster times than the trams some of the services were run non-stop between London Road High Level and Daybrook. With their

Thorneywood station looking disused and neglected, but with the infra-structure still intact. The footbridge was removed in 1930 so this picture dates from before that year. (Courtesy of Nottingham City Council Leisure and Community Services Central Library Local Studies Library)

comparatively light loads and the easy acceleration afforded by electric traction the trams could negotiate the gradients in the hilly east of Nottingham more easily than steam locomotives. A particular problem for the latter was the 1 in 49 gradient, which was also on a steep curve, rising from the Trent Lane junction.

Supposedly as a wartime economy measure Thorneywood, St Ann's Well and Sherwood stations were closed to passengers on 13th July 1916, and the line thereafter was used only by two trains a day running from Nottingham to Shirebrook on the Great Northern's Leen Valley line. Needless to say the stations were not permanently reopened to passengers after the war.

However, in 1928 there was a temporary revival. King George V and Queen Mary were visiting Nottingham. Their programme included opening the Royal Show at Wollaton Park, appearing before 17,500 Nottingham schoolchildren in Woodthorpe Park, and opening the new University College complex at Highfields (later to become Nottingham University). The closest railway station to Woodthorpe Park was Sherwood, so both Thorneywood and Sherwood stations were renovated and re-staffed for the occasion. This made it possible to bring in 6,550 of the children, with 284 teachers, in 13 special trains running to Sherwood from Basford & Bulwell, Thorneywood and Nottingham Low Level stations. So Thorneywood and Sherwood stations on that one day (10th July 1928) saw more activity than on any other previous occasion in their history.

In 1930 the down line was removed and the Nottingham Suburban Railway became single track. The station footbridges were then removed, a clear indication that the stations would never be reopened. Through services were maintained until January 1931, but thereafter the line was used solely for goods traffic with only St Ann's Well station remaining open for goods handling.

The next misfortune to the line occurred on the night of 8th/9th May 1941. In Nottingham's worst air raid of the war a bomb landed in the southern section, damaging a bridge over the LMS line and blowing away part of the embankment. The damage was never repaired, and buffers were placed at the end of the northern and southern sections of the line, which now became dead-ends. For the rest of the war and after the lines

Sneinton tunnel was for a time was used as a rifle range, but is now bricked up. This is the northern portal. (Author)

were used to store old railway wagons, and some local residents believed (erroneously) that these were there as a decoy for the Luftwaffe.

Freight trains, latterly carrying only domestic coal, continued to use the section between Daybrook and Thorneywood. This traffic, however, stopped on 1st August 1951. The last passenger train to run over the line, between Daybrook and Thorneywood and back, was a chartered rail enthusiasts' special on 16th June 1951. In the following years the track was removed as were the lattice steel bridges, which had been a feature of the line. Later most of the various brick bridges were demolished. Embankments were removed, some of the spoil being used to fill the

91

The old railway embankment carrying the public footpath comes to an abrupt end here. The embankment has been removed to make way for an industrial estate. The path is diverted to a new route to the left of the picture. (Author)

tunnels. Sneinton tunnel was for a time used as a rifle range, but eventually was bricked up.

Few people in Nottingham now know that the line was there, and we needed the help of local historian Stephen Best to trace what relics still remain. The longest stretch of the old trackbed of the Nottingham Suburban Railway still extant, where it passes through Sneinton, has been made into a footpath.

7

Parallel Lines, Rival Stations

Duplication in the Leen Valley

Midland Railway stations	Great Northern Railway stations	Great Central Railway stations
Basford Vernon	Basford & Bulwell	New Basford
Bulwell Market	Bulwell Forest	Bulwell Common
Hucknall Byron	Hucknall Town	Hucknall Central
Sutton-in-Ashfield and Sutton Junction	Sutton-in-Ashfield Town	Sutton-in-Ashfield Central

Four small Nottinghamshire townships, all in the Leen Valley, with thirteen stations between them.

This is what happens when competing railway companies, furious in their rivalry, lay down lines running almost parallel to one another.

This is what happened in Nottinghamshire's Leen Valley.

The River Leen is not a large river, by any standard, and for much of its length is little more than a wide stream. The same could be said of the River Erewash, over to its west. Both rise in the Robin Hood Hills, near Kirkby-in-Ashfield. The importance of these two little rivers is that their valleys have given their names to two important coalfields, which stimulated much of the railway development in Nottinghamshire.

The Midland Railway, as so often happened in the county, was there first. It had already created its lines between Nottingham and Derby, Nottingham and Leicester, and Nottingham and Lincoln. It had no hesitation in pushing its lines up the Erewash Valley (see Chapter 9) and the Leen Valley.

The first stretch of the Midland's Leen Valley line, from Lenton Junction to Kirkby, was opened on 2nd October 1848. It included the important engineering work of the Annesley tunnel through the Robin Hood Hills. Going from south to north, as it was

93

Kirkby-in-Ashfield station on the former Midland Railway's Leen Valley line, a picture taken on 2nd September 1955. British Railways London Midland region locomotive 41947 is pulling away with the 4.40 pm stopping train to Whitwell. (H.C. Casserley, Berkhamsted)

constructed, the line leaves the original 1839 Nottingham to Derby line in a sweeping curve. There was a Lenton station but this was closed in 1911, as a result of the introduction from 1900 onwards of electric tram services. The clanging bells of the trams often sounded the death knell of suburban stations, as we saw in Chapter 6.

The next station was Radford, of which nothing remains, except that differently-coloured brickwork on the bridge on Ilkeston Road shows where once an entrance led to a flight of steps going to the down platform. After that came Basford Vernon station (Basford until 1952), which was closed in 1960 and later demolished. The thoroughfare Vernon Road was actually built by the Midland Railway so that traffic did not have to keep criss-crossing the railway line.

The route goes through Bulwell and out into the country, past Hucknall, Linby, Newstead (Newstead Abbey was the ancestral home of Lord Byron the poet) and as far as Sutton Junction in the coalfield.

94

An engraving of Lenton station as it was in 1850, shortly after the opening of the Midland Railway Leen Valley line. (Courtesy of Nottingham City Council Leisure and Community Services Central Library Local Studies Library)

The same station 50 years later. More buildings have been erected, though the original pair with gable ends appear to be still there. The level crossing has been replaced by a road bridge. (Courtesy of Nottingham City Council Leisure and Community Services Central Library Local Studies Library)

Sutton Junction station (Midland Railway) some time in the early 20th century, with the landmark Aldington's Mill. (Courtesy of Nottingham City Council Leisure and Community Services Central Library Local Studies Library)

Although the initial motive for the line was to serve the coalmines of the Leen Valley, the Midland Railway also set out to attract passenger traffic. With this in mind the opening was timed to coincide with Nottingham's Goose Fair, an annual event held during the first week of October, which was then, and still is, the country's largest temporary fair. Even before railways huge numbers of people, some from a considerable distance away, would travel to Nottingham for the occasion. The railways, however, reinforced its popularity.

During that Goose Fair week in October 1848 there were no fewer than 20 services a day on the new line. Passengers from Mansfield, still some distance north of the terminus, were invited to use specially-made, horse-drawn transport on the Mansfield to Kirkby section of the old Mansfield to Pinxton horse railway, but the demand far exceeded the supply, and most of the Mansfield fairgoers had to make their way to the railhead on foot. After the fair was over the Midland Railway set to work to convert the

The Midland Railway's station at Mansfield in 1919. (From an old postcard)

section of that old horse-drawn railway which lay between Kirkby and Mansfield to make it usable for steam locomotion. The lower section of the Mansfield to Pinxton horse railway was also later converted for steam locomotives, and is still in use today.

The Leen Valley line reached Mansfield, the biggest town in Nottinghamshire apart from Nottingham itself, a year later, on 9th October 1849. The line was extended towards Worksop in 1875, mainly to foil Great Northern ambitions to build a line from Retford (on their main line between London and the north) to Mansfield.

The Midland enjoyed its monopoly for over 30 years, and was able to ignore complaints that its trains were slow (stopping trains taking about 50 minutes for the 17¼ mile journey from Nottingham to Mansfield), none too clean, and subject to delays owing to the heavy coal traffic also using the line. Even as late as the 1950s the problem was how to fit all the coal trains round the passenger services, and vice versa.

During the First World War and for many years after there were special trains over this line taking munitions workers from

97

Hucknall Town station on the former Great Northern line around 1930. (Stations UK, Southport)

Mansfield and stations on the line to the giant Royal Ordnance factory at Chilwell.

The Midland's monopoly came to an end in 1882, when the Great Northern opened its own Leen Valley line, from Bulwell, where there was a junction with the GNR's Derbyshire Extension line, to Newstead. Once again its prime objective was to muscle in on the coal trade, and every major coalmine in the valley was eventually to have both Midland and Great Northern branches running into its yards. There were many places where Midland and Great Northern tracks were running parallel, less than a quarter of a mile apart, and occasionally side by side. At the mining town of Hucknall they criss-crossed one another twice.

Great Northern passenger trains ran between Nottingham London Road station and Newstead as soon as the line was open, with intermediate stations at Bestwood, Butler's Hill, Hucknall and Linby. The line was later extended to serve Annesley Colliery.

An additional station, Bulwell Forest, opened in 1887. This was very basic, with a wooden platfom. There were few passengers, the station having been built for the Duke of St Albans, who owned the nearby Bestwood Estate (now a country park). One of those myths that seem to attach themselves so readily to out-of-the-way railway stations was that Bulwell Forest was really built so that Great Northern directors could use it to go and play golf at the Bulwell Forest golf course. The story cannot be true, for the station pre-dated the golf course, but it is still often repeated.

Then, at the very end of the 19th century yet another set of railway lines was laid down the Leen Valley. This time it was the great Great Central Railway, which, as we saw in Chapter 1, was pushing southwards with its main line to London.

This is why some of those small townships came to have three railway stations. In the case of Basford not only was New Basford station on the Great Central line only 1,000 yards away from Basford Vernon station on the Midland line, with a Great Northern station at Basford & Bulwell, but there was also Basford & Bulwell station on the Great Northern's Derbyshire Extension line, the Back Line described in Chapter 4.

Linby was the first to lose its Great Northern passenger service, as early as 1916. In the inter-war years the Great Northern's Leen Valley line was fighting a losing battle for

Hucknall Central station on the Great Central line, again in the early 1930s. (Stations UK, Southport)

99

passengers not only with the parallel Midland and Great Central routes but also because of motor buses.

Coal freight trains kept this Great Northern line open for another 30 years, but then, when rationalisation became the order of the day, there was no way the authorities were going to allow three parallel sets of tracks to survive. We saw in Chapter 1 how the Great Central line disappeared along its entire length, including the Leen Valley section, and the same thing happened to the Great Northern. The stations were closed and the lines taken up.

Sutton-in-Ashfield could at one time boast four stations (if we include Sutton Junction which was outside the town). The Great Northern closed its Leen Valley stations, including Sutton-in-Ashfield Town, to passengers in 1931, but the former Great Central and Midland stations survived until nationalisation and British Railways. When in the 1950s British Railways decided to withdraw passenger services calling at the former Great Central station of Sutton-in-Ashfield Central, they reopened that old Great Northern station (despite it having been closed to passengers for 25 years) to run services to Nottingham Victoria.

Sutton-in-Ashfield Central station in 1948. (Stations UK, Southport)

However, the facility was not well patronised and closed again after a few months.

The forthcoming withdrawal of all passenger services on the Midland's Leen Valley line was announced in November 1963, which was 11 months before the service actually ended. The last day of passenger trains was 10th October 1964, and no one thought that passenger services would ever be run again on the line. The Midland lines continued to remain open, but only for mineral traffic.

Following the closure of this and the other lines Mansfield, with its population of 60,000, shared with Gosport in Hampshire the dubious honour of being the largest towns in Great Britain not to have a direct railway passenger service. However, on 7th May 1973, a new station did open called Alfreton & Mansfield Parkway, on the Nottingham–Leeds line, with financial contributions from eleven local authorities. As its name suggests it has a large car park, and there are connecting bus services to Mansfield, Kirkby-in-Ashfield and Sutton-in-Ashfield, but Alfreton & Mansfield Parkway station is 8 miles away from Mansfield, and, to add insult to injury, actually located over the county boundary in Derbyshire.

British Rail's idea was to keep the Leen Valley line open for coal traffic. However, the coalfield and mines along the line were then in decline. Babbington, Annesley, Sherwood and Warsop collieries, all with links to the line, have closed since 1981. Newstead Colliery closed in 1987 and others are threatened with closure. The line north of Newstead to Kirkby-in-Ashfield was abandoned altogether, but the link from the Midland main line to Kirkby-in-Ashfield and across the town on a fine viaduct to Mansfield Woodhouse and then on to Worksop was retained for freight.

On 17th October 1982 a meeting took place between the Railway Development Society and Mansfield District Council about the possibility of restoring passenger services to Mansfield. There was enthusiasm but lack of funding. But in 1988 the Nottinghamshire County Council commissioned a study, carried out by the University of Leeds, which concluded that there was considerable potential demand for a revived service from a catchment area of 300,000 people. British Rail agreed to go ahead

Mansfield station in 2004, four years after it was brought back into use. The down platform. (Rodger Smith)

with the venture with some assistance from local authorities, and the line was given the name 'Robin Hood Line'.

A service from Nottingham to Newstead opened on 17th May 1993, with a station at Hucknall. Bulwell station opened a year later. Passenger services were extended from Newstead to Mansfield Woodhouse (north of Mansfield) on 20th November 1995, with stations at Sutton Parkway, Mansfield and Mansfield Woodhouse (the old goods shed was converted to a passenger station). Kirkby station was added a year later. The service from Mansfield Woodhouse to Worksop reopened for passengers on 25th May 1998, with new stations at Shirebrook, Langwith-Whaley Thorns, Cresswell and Whitwell.

The original Mansfield station building was brought back into use as a result of a major restoration project, and on 2nd February 2001 John Meade, a former booking clerk with British Rail, who had sold the last ticket at Mansfield before the 1964

The railway heritage is suitably celebrated in the inn sign at a public house, the Midland, not far from Mansfield station. (Rodger Smith)

closure, was brought back to sell the first ticket from the refurbished station.

Mansfield railway historians Paul Anderson and Jack Cupit have worked out that in the two miles of the Robin Hood Line between Kirkby tunnel (the most expensive piece of new engineering on the line) and Sutton Parkway station, the train uses trackbeds or track alignments from the Midland Railway dating from 1848; Railtrack dating from 1995; the Great Central (then still called the Manchester, Sheffield and Lincolnshire) dating from 1892, though now raised by 30 feet; the Great Northern dating from 1896, though now partly above it); British Rail from 1972; and the Mansfield & Pinxton (originally horse-drawn) railway dating back to 1819. As they have written: 'The story ranges from horse-drawn wagons during the times of George III, to Turbostars well into the reign of Elizabeth II.'

Part of the Bulwell to Hucknall footpath using the trackbed of the old Great Northern Leen Valley line. This cutting was just past Bulwell Forest station, of which no trace remains. (Author)

104

Lost lines, the Robin Hood Line has shown, may not remain lost lines for ever.

Some of the trackbed of the closed Great Northern line, between Bulwell and Hucknall, has been turned into a footpath. To access it, take a Robin Hood Line train (or the new Nottingham tram service) to Bulwell station, look for the church, and exit in that direction, by steps up to a road. Turn into Church Lane, and where this reduces to a footpath turn right up some steps to Northholme Avenue. Follow this street dowhill and turn left at the bottom into Cantrell Road. Walk to the end of Cantrell Road, and its T-junction with St Alban's Road. Cross over to a path between houses that leads to Bulwell Forest golf course. As you approach the golf course, turn sharp left (at the end of the houses) up some steps set in a grass bank, then climb steadily to a broad green track enclosed by hedges and then by a cutting. You are now on the trackbed. At the end of the cutting the path descends to a path that skirts the golf course. Follow this, and you will have the trackbed embankment on your left. When you come to a main road (Hucknall Road), you cross this and enter a wood. The path then climbs to the top of the old railway embankment (SK 547466) and uses the embankment for over a mile.

8

The Southwell Paddy

The Rural Line for Mid-Nottinghamshire

The Southwell Paddy in service between Southwell station and Rolleston Junction. (Frank Ashley, courtesy of the Midland Railway Centre, Butterley, Derbyshire)

Quiet village stations with porters spending much of their time handling milk churns. Homely little engines recognisable to everyone who lived by the line. A time where no one seemed to be in a hurry. The nearest Nottinghamshire came to this idyllic picture of a vanished world was during the heyday of the Southwell to Mansfield Railway.

Southwell is a quiet rural township 15 miles from Nottingham,

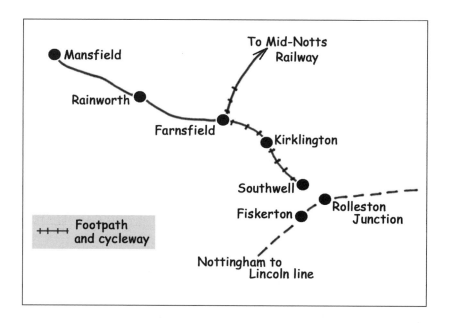

with strong ecclesiastical connections and dominated by Southwell Minster. There is no Anglican cathedral in Nottingham itself (which often surprises visitors) and the city and most of Nottinghamshire lies in the diocese of Southwell.

The town was first connected up to the railway network by means of a short (2½ miles) branch from Rolleston Junction (then called Southwell Junction), on the Nottingham to Lincoln line. This opened on 1st July 1847. Steam locomotives were used, but the take-up on the service was so poor that they were replaced by horses from 1853 to 1860, with an eventual reduction to one horse-drawn train a week, as far as Fiskerton station as there was then no station at the junction itself. By 1860 the Midland Railway was getting worried by the threat of competition, and steam locomotives were restored in September 1860, and a station created at Rolleston Junction. The MR then began to consider extending the line all the way to Mansfield, but when no action seemed to be forthcoming a Southwell businessman, John Barrow, told the Midland directors that if they were not going to build the line, he would construct one himself.

107

The Midland, always sensitive to anything that might be construed as competition, and certainly not wanting any interloper between two of its established railheads, thereupon jerked into life. The line was constructed as single-track with passing places. The opportunity was also taken to rebuild Southwell station in stone (the earlier timber structure being dismantled and taken to Beeston to be re-erected). Passenger services started on 3rd April 1871, passing through the very heart of Sherwood Forest, with stations at Kirklington, Farnsfield (the village which claims the burial place of Robin Hood's henchman Will Scarlett) and Rainworth.

From when it was built until the First World War this was a vital lifeline to the isolated villages along its route. In the days before motor transport everything, from the post to domestic furniture, came in by the railway, which then took away the local farm produce. It was indeed one of the principal tasks of the porters at these village stations to handle the many milk churns – and one of the trains was in fact called 'The Milk Train', though it carried a miscellany of farm produce as well as milk.

The Southwell to Mansfield route, being very rural, had the reputation of being something of a leisurely line, and drivers and firemen of goods trains were said to amuse and feed themselves by catching rabbits. One story is that they threw lumps of coal at them, but the weapon was more likely a gun hidden in their locker.

In 1884, when the bishopric of Southwell was created, and the new bishop was due to arrive, employees of the Midland Railway artistically decorated Southwell station with flags and bunting.

In the later 1880s one train from Southwell to Mansfield then went on to Ambergate and Buxton. It had to take such a roundabout route that its average speed worked out at 15 mph, and the service consequently had few takers and did not last long. Some railway histories mention the story – another of those railway myths – that as Buxton was by way of being the furthest outpost in the diocese of Southwell the train had been put on at the behest of the Bishop. This, however, is unlikely. At this time the Bishop was resident in Thurgarton, the Bishop's Manor at Southwell not being built until 1907.

108

Farnsfield station in 1948, with the station buildings still intact, though by this time they were used only for goods traffic. The goods shed building in the background is still there, next to the car park for the Southwell Trail footpath. The station house is now a private residence. (Stations UK, Southport)

The Farnsfield station goods warehouse today. (Judy Kingscott)

Southwell station reached its busiest year in 1899, when the number of passenger bookings at the station reached 29,542. One of the biggest occasions ever seen at the station was on Monday, 10th July 1901, when a wounded Boer War hero, Major L.E. Starkey, a member of a local squire's family, was due to come home. His horse travelled on the same train. Residents of Southwell, complete with a brass band, gathered at the station to meet the major. Great interest was shown in the horse, which had carried the major through his campaigns.

After the First World War there were two or three trains a day on the Mansfield–Southwell section, with an extra one on Thursday, this being market day in Mansfield, an important consideration for the farms on the route. Some 20 trains a day each way ran from Southwell to the main line and on to Nottingham or Newark. However, the emphasis changed as new collieries opened up at Blidworth, in 1926, and Bilsthorpe, in 1928. And it was in 1928 that the number of coalmines in Britain reached its peak. There was now so much freight traffic on the line that the section from Southwell to Rolleston Junction was made double track.

But the coming of motor transport ended the rural isolation of Kirklington, Farnsfield and Rainworth, and passenger business at these stations dropped to uneconomic levels. They were closed to passengers as early as 1929, the last train running on 12th August 1929. One reason for the uncompetitive nature of the passenger services was the slowness of the trains (which sometimes took 40 minutes for the 12½ miles from Southwell to Mansfield), partly because of the heavy mineral traffic on the line.

The most persistent legend of this line, repeated in various books and leaflets, is that it was possible to get off at any of the village stations, stroll to the public house, down a pint, and get back to the station in time to catch the same train. Mansfield railway historian Jack Cupit checked the November 1876 timetable, and found that the 12.43 pm from Kirklington was not due to depart from Farnsfield, the next station on the line, until 1.30 pm. The rail journey between the two stations took five minutes, so there could have been 42 minutes to get a drink at Farnsfield!

110

Exterior of Southwell station,1955. (H.C. Casserley, Berkhamsted)

When a new line (the Mid-Notts Joint Railway) was opened in 1930 between Farnsfield and Ollerton, to serve more collieries and even an oil well at Eakring, there was never any question of providing a passenger service or station. The stations at Blidworth, Farnsfield and Kirklington, however, were kept open for goods traffic until 1964.

The LMS, successor to the Midland Railway, obviously knew of the adage 'If you can't beat 'em, join 'em', and entered into an agreement with the Mansfield Tramways company to run a joint bus service between Mansfield, Southwell and Newark, calling at Rainworth, Farnsfield and Kirklington. Although the intermediate stations remained closed, there were occasional passenger trains running between Mansfield and to or through Southwell, these being either race-day specials (Southwell has a well-known horse-racing course) or seaside specials.

Southwell was kept open as a commuter station, but now with hardly any through trains. Passengers were henceforth expected to change at Rolleston Junction. The service between Southwell and Rolleston Junction was provided by the Southwell Paddy, a fondly remembered single-coach train that went backwards and forwards between the two places. With the journey being so

Southwell station in 1948, taken from the up platform. (Stations UK, Southport)

The down platform of Southwell station in 1948. (Stations UK, Southport)

short there was no need for constant stoking of the boiler, and it was apparently not unknown for the driver to let his fireman off the train so he could collect mushrooms from the field beside the track, and then pick him up on the return journey.

The *Oxford English Dictionary* defines one of the senses of 'Paddy' as 'a train for conveying coal from a pithead', but in Nottinghamshire generally the term was used for regular trains which did not appear in the regular timetables, but were put on in various places solely to take coalminers to the various collieries. A large proportion of Nottinghamshire, as readers of this book will by now have gathered, is practically built on coal. In Southwell, however, the term was simply an affectionate epithet for its local shuttle service.

The locomotive most regularly used for the Paddy, British Railways number 58065, was a truly venerable survivor, a Johnson 0-4-4T, which dated it back to the pre-1923 Grouping Midland Railway. It was certainly the last working engine in its class.

The Paddy did not run on Sundays. The timetable for the weekday service in the summer of 1958 stated 'Steam service', and had 17 departures from Southwell to Rolleston Junction between 6.33 am and 9.20 pm, with corresponding return journeys. On Saturdays there were extra trains. The journey took five minutes.

There is a well-attested story that when a Southwell notary called Kenneth Tweedale-Meaby became Clerk to the Nottinghamshire County Council, and hence a commuter, he had an informal arrangement with the station staff that the morning Paddy, which then left at 8.55, would not depart from Southwell until he was aboard. One day it went without him, and he insisted on the mainline train waiting at Rolleston Junction while the Paddy came back and fetched him.

However, on 10th January 1955 the engine shed at Southwell where the venerable locomotive was housed was closed, and the engine moved to Newark. Many people then realised that the end was in sight, and the Southwell Paddy was finally withdrawn from service in June 1959, despite a petition signed by 350 people. No 58065 had been withdrawn from service in April that year and for the last three months the Paddy was

113

drawn by any engine that could be found. After services ended a sign was erected at Rolleston Junction, 'Alight here for Southwell'. In earlier times, up to the closure of the stations between Southwell and Mansfield, the signs had read 'Rolleston Junction, for Southwell and Mansfield Branch'.

Freight services (including a local pick-up train which collected individual loads from the stations still acting as goods stations) continued to operate over the line until 1st March 1965, but after that the station buildings were either demolished or sold for private use. Between 1965 and 1968 the National Coal Board took over the line, using it for colliery traffic. After that the section between Blidworth and Rolleston Junction was closed completely, and the rails were taken up. The section between Blidworth and Mansfield was used for a few more years by the National Coal Board, before being gradually sold off for development.

However, the trackbed of the section between Farnsfield and Southwell was acquired by the Nottinghamshire County Council in 1969 and designated as a public footpath, known as the Southwell Trail. The conversion to a footpath was part of the council's programme for European Conservation Year. The opening day for the footpath was 30th March 1970, with a ceremony at Farnsfield.

The Southwell Trail, 7½ miles of it, is the longest continuous stretch of Nottinghamshire's lost railways that is fully open to the public for walking or riding (cycles or horses). Car parks and picnic sites are provided on or near the sites of old stations at Southwell (SK 705545), Kirklington (676567) and Farnsfield (646574). There is also a helpful leaflet with a large illustration of locomotive 58065.

In a letter to the author in February 2004 Pete Jarman, Recreational Routes Officer for Nottinghamshire County Council, wrote that the authority would always consider buying a redundant railway to enhance or provide public access. 'It may be worth noting some of the really lost lines, such as the extension towards Mansfield of what could have been part of the Southwell Trail. I know it is with the benefit of hindsight that we can look at the lost opportunities. I am sure that folk, post-Beeching, were overwhelmed with all of those lines becoming

The start of the Southwell Trail, at Farnsfield, facing in the direction of Southwell. Another path, along the trackbed of the old Mid-Notts line to Bilsthorpe, goes off to the left. (Author)

redundant virtually overnight. If only Beeching's closures were happening now. What a network of Trails we could have!'

Apart from the trackbed itself and bridges where it is crossed by roads or farm access tracks, there are hardly any railway artefacts left. The station houses at Southwell, Kirklington and Farnsfield have been turned into private houses.

The Southwell end of the trail is at a car park (SK 705545) close to the site of Southwell station, which was on the opposite side of the road which here crosses the railway trackbed at right angles. However, east of the official trail the route of the track between Southwell and Rolleston Junction can be traced in parts (some of it is now an access road to the racecourse). Going back to the start of the trail, there can be seen (and visited by the thirsty) the Newcastle Arms, on one side of the car park. This public house was originally built for the convenience of railway travellers.

115

An unusual feature of walking the trackbed is how straight parts of the line are. In particular the section between Southwell until just short of Kirklington runs straight as a ruler, and approaching walkers or cyclists, particularly if they are wearing bright clothing, can be made out more than a mile away.

Between Southwell and Kirklington is Maythorne crossing. Although there was a bridge here under the railway embankment, it proved not high enough for farm carts if they were loaded high (at mowing or harvest time) with hay or corn. It was impossible to increase the height so, an unusual feature, a supplementary crossing, was provided as well as the bridge. Between Kirklington and Farnsfield the track rises to an embankment, pierced by a high bridge (actually called High Bridge) leading to the isolated Springs Farm. This time it was possible to make the bridge tall enough to allow the passage of those troublesome hay and corn loads.

At Farnsfield there is the junction with the Mid-Notts line to Eakring and Ollerton, which forms a two-mile extension to the footpath. Next to the car park at Farnsfield the old goods shed still stands (which since closure of the line has had various uses, one being to store pantomime scenery).

After Farnsfield the more determined walkers (we are now off the section maintained by the County Council) can push on further along the trackbed, on a stretch much used by farm vehicles. After a point where these vehicles turn into the fields there is a short stretch densely overgrown with brambles, though a pathway through is still practicable, until it comes to an abrupt end at a point where traffic on the A614 trunk road (SK 627574) thunders past below. The bridge which here carried the railway over the road has of course long since disappeared.

From here on in the direction of Mansfield there is no longer a continuous traceable line. At one point a short stretch of embankment in a farmer's field can be glimpsed from the Farnsfield to Rainworth road. But in Mansfield itself a section of nearly 3 miles has been converted by the Mansfield Council into a walking and cycling track. Called the Mansfield Way, it was formally opened on 30th April 1987. It is, however, difficult to get the feel of a railway, since it swoops up and down with bewildering changes of level. A long-term resident, a former

In Mansfield the line of the Southwell to Mansfield railway was converted in 1987 to a walking and cycling track called the Mansfield Way. (Judy Kingscott)

railwayman, who was walking his dog along the path when your author was checking out this path, confirmed that a great deal of earth-moving had taken place in past years, partly because of subsidence, partly because of the removal of bridges, and partly because of the need to level ground for new building, and all this had drastically changed the contours. But though the gradients have changed, the route follows faithfully the course of one of the most attractive of our lost lines.

117

9
North And West Nottinghamshire

Erewash Valley Line
Basford to Bennerley Junction
Pleasley Vale (Alfreton to Mansfield)
The Penny Emma
Leen Valley Extension
The Mansfield Railway

Erewash Valley Line

The River Erewash forms, for much of its course, the western boundary of Nottinghamshire, dividing it from Derbyshire. However, the Erewash Valley coalfield lies both sides of the county boundary, and railway lines snake backwards and forwards.

This is particularly true of the Midland Railway's Erewash Valley line, opened in 1847, which follows the course of the river. The line is still open, but all the passenger stations along it were condemned in the Beeching report and closed on 12th October 1964. Nearly all of them were demolished leaving little trace. We can, therefore, include it in this book as a line lost to passenger traffic.

The stations were, in order going from south to north: Long Eaton, Stapleford & Sandiacre, Stanton Gate, Trowell, Ilkeston Junction, Langley Mill & Eastwood, Codnor Park & Ironville, Pye Bridge, Alfreton & Normanton, Westhouses & Blackwell, and Clay Cross.

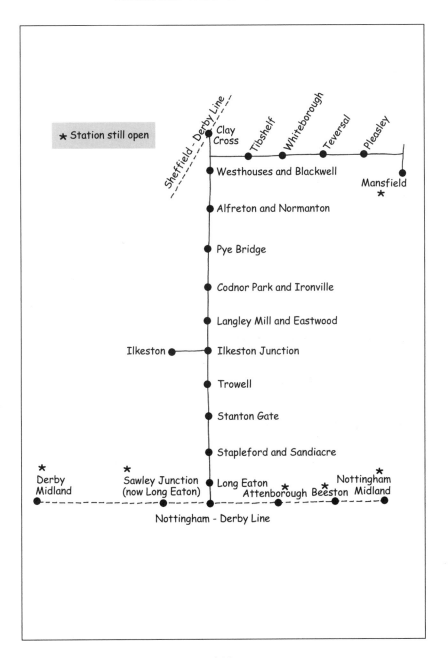

Station signs – this particular design is called a totem – showing the complete run of stations on a journey from Nottingham, including every station on the Erewash Valley line, part of the impressive collection of memorabilia expert Brian Amos. (Judy Kingscott)

After Long Eaton station closed the 'Long Eaton' name was transferred to a station on the Nottingham to Derby line previously called Sawley Junction. Before the First World War there were regular scheduled services from Nottingham to Stanton Gate and back to bring and fetch hundreds of workers to and from the mighty Stanton Ironworks.

In 1951 Trowell station was particularly busy, since Trowell, out of all the villages in the country, had been named the Festival of Britain village. The choice has puzzled everyone then and since, but the community can now boast a large public house called the Festival Inn.

Ilkeston in Derbyshire is the largest town on the line. It had been bypassed by this Midland Railway Erewash Valley line, but this did not seem to matter until the Great Northern's Derbyshire Extension line (see Chapter 4) passed through the middle of Ilkeston and put it firmly on the railway map. All the Midland could do then was to run a shuttle service from its own town centre station (the site is now occupied by a bus garage) to an Ilkeston Junction station on the other side of the river Erewash, and therefore in Nottinghamshire. Ilkeston's little branch line was never very successful, most Ilkestonians preferring to travel to Nottingham or Derby by the much more practical Great

Ilkeston Junction station, a picture taken in the 1930s. (Stations UK, Southport)

Northern line, and the Ilkeston town centre station closed as early as 1947. By parking at Cossall Common (SK 476434) one can take a walk along the footpath alongside the Nottingham Canal, now a nature reserve. Southwards one can take a look at Ilkeston Junction station (SK 476424), and northwards the Bennerley viaduct, mentioned in Chapter 4.

There is, encouragingly, a new station at Langley Mill, opened, with local government financial support, in 1986, and trains running between Nottingham and Sheffield sometimes stop there. Before privatisation the possibility of opening more stations on the Erewash Valley line was being looked at, but these ideas seem to have been lost without trace.

Basford to Bennerley Junction

A Midland Railway line that is completely lost is one from Basford on its Leen Valley line to Bennerley Junction on the Erewash Valley line. As so often in Nottinghamshire the initial motive for the line was coal, and particularly to gain access to the Watnall Colliery. However, the opportunity was not lost to try to get back some passenger traffic from the Great Northern's Derbyshire Extension line.

From 1882 the Midland Railway even used the Basford–Bennerley line to try to retrieve some of its Ilkeston business by running six passenger trains each way direct from the town centre station the along the line to Basford, but these ceased to run during the First World War and were never reinstated. After this service ceased there seemed no point in maintaining the line beyond the point where it served the collieries and Kimberley station. West of Kimberley station, therefore, the lines were taken up and shipped to France to build troop railways there. Railway histories have stated that the ship was torpedoed and its cargo lost, though your author and his advisers have not been able to trace the source of this story.

Kimberley station was closed to passengers in 1917 but remained open for handling goods until 1st January 1951. It was then converted into a social club. Watnall station also closed to passengers in 1917, and to goods in 1954, but its site has now been lost to development.

Pleasley Vale (Alfreton to Mansfield)

As mentioned in Chapter 7, between the Beeching closures in the 1960s and the opening of the Robin Hood Line in 1990s Mansfield was one of the two largest towns in England without direct access to a passenger rail service. This was particularly odd, since at the beginning of the 20th century it had been at the hub of a complicated web of railway lines, and Mansfield's Midland station had more passenger trains on a weekday than London St Pancras.

Although the lines radiating out from Mansfield were established primarily to fetch coal from the many coalmines and distribute it throughout the country via the large marshalling yards at Colwick and Toton, passenger services were important too. Every coalmine generated employment, and the mining settlements that sprang up in the 19th century quickly grew into little townships. These were so numerous that they practically adjoined one another. This is one reason why so many of the stations have 'double-barrelled' names, such as Codnor Park & Ironville, Westhouses & Blackwell and so on. Another reason is that the lines were built primarily to serve collieries, and the routes rarely went through town centres. Yet until the era of motor transport got underway after the First World War, the residents of these townships depended on the railway network to get them about.

One such line left the Erewash Valley line at a junction at Westhouses and extended to serve a string of coalmines, firstly to Teversal, then to Pleasley and then on to form a junction with the Mansfield to Worksop line near Mansfield Woodhouse. When the link was completed a passenger train service could then start, in 1886, between Mansfield and Alfreton serving a number of these colliery towns, and connections with mainline trains were made at Alfreton. However, such a service was susceptible to competition from motor buses, and the Midland Railway's

Sutton-in-Ashfield station (Midland Railway) in the middle of the town at the opening in 1893. The Sutton Council poses for a picture on the platform (though one small individual looks too young to be a councillor!).

successor, the LMS, withdrew scheduled passenger services in 1930. The stations at Teversal and Pleasley closed at this time, though they remained open for goods traffic until 1963. A particularly remote station, at Whiteborough (between Tibshelf and Teversal), had closed to all traffic as early as 1926.

The line was still open until recently for coal traffic from Westhouses to Teversal Colliery, but the rest of the line was abandoned and the rails taken up. Fortunately the latter section was the prettiest part of the line, following the valley of the River Meden and passing through the attractive countryside of the Pleasley Vale. Here again the Nottinghamshire County Council, working in close co-operation with the Derbyshire County Council and the district local authorities, has created attractive footpaths, the Teversal Trail and the Meden Trail, making full use of the old trackbeds. Full details can be obtained from the Teversal Trail Visitor Centre, Carnarvon Street, Fackley Road, Teversal, Sutton-in-Ashfield, NG17 3HJ; telephone 01623 442021; grid reference SK 480617. The trails radiating out from here also include the Rowthorne Trail, following another Midland Railway line opened in the 1870s to service a number of collieries between Pleasley and Bolsover, and which was then used to run passenger services between Mansfield and Chesterfield. This line (mostly in Derbyshire) closed in the 1930s.

The area around the visitor centre at Teversal, once crowded with smoky coalmines and a complex network of colliery railways and sidings, has now been landscaped into extensive parkland, with one of the walks taking you up to the highest point in Nottinghamshire, allowing good views over to Hardwick Hall, an Elizabethan mansion across the county boundary in Derbyshire. There are various free leaflets available, but the one called *Pleasley Trails – Industrial Heritage* is the one that clearly shows the relationship of the trails to the old railway lines.

The Penny Emma

Sutton-in-Ashfield had been bypassed by the Midland Railway's

Nottingham to Mansfield Leen Valley line, but in 1893 the Midland Railway built a branch from a new station, called Sutton Junction, on the Leen Valley line to run to a new terminus in the town centre. Journeys between the two were made by a little shuttle service. As we saw with Southwell in Chapter 8, such shuttles attracted diminutives or nicknames, and this particular one was always known locally as the Penny Emma. The town centre station closed to passengers in 1949, though unadvertised workmen's trains continued to run from there for a further two years. The station closed finally on 1st October 1951, and it is now difficult to trace the course of the line to Sutton Junction (which closed post-Beeching, in 1964).

Leen Valley Extension

The Midland Railway had little choice but to create this awkward shuttle, because it had become aware that shortly Sutton-in-Ashfield was no longer going to be bypassed. Planning to come right into the middle of the town was the Great Northern with its

Skegby station in 1948. (Stations UK, Southport)

Sutton-in-Ashfield Town station.

Leen Valley Extension line, opened for passenger traffic between 1898 and 1901. From Annesley the Great Northern made use of its running powers over Great Central lines to Kirkby South Junction. From this junction it then thrust northwards into Sutton-in-Ashfield, where an important-looking station, built in the local limestone, was created. The line continued to run northwards to Skegby (where the former station site has now been landscaped) and on to Teversal, crossing the Midland Alfreton to Mansfield line, and into the Derbyshire side of the coalfield.

From a passenger point of view, however, the line, though heavily engineered and therefore expensive to create, was never very successful apart from special trains run for miners. When bus transport developed into a serious competitor it obviously became uneconomic, and services were withdrawn in 1931.

The line remained open for coal traffic, but when this declined there was surplus railway capacity, and the old Midland Leen Valley line was now able to cope. The Great Northern line was therefore abandoned. Within Nottinghamshire its embankments can still be traced between Skegby and Pleasley (grid references: SK 495615 to 500643).

The Mansfield Railway

One of the last lines to be built in Nottinghamshire, and one of the last general services (passengers and goods) railways to be built in Britain, was the Mansfield Railway. It was constructed in the early years of the 20th century when new coalmines, the so-called deep mines, which were on a larger scale than the 19th century mines, were being opened up in the vicinity of Mansfield itself. There was promise of heavy traffic, and investors still did not take seriously the competition from the motor vehicle when it came to moving passengers. The railway was initiated by a group of coalowners and Mansfield businessmen after attempts to interest two of the three railway companies already operating in the area, the Great Northern and Great Central, had failed (they did not approach the Midland Railway since the Midland was already too well-entrenched and it was felt that their coal freight charges were too high). In fact during the 1890s there was a body called the Mansfield Railway Commissioners, which lobbied existing companies for better services and was always looking into possible new connections.

The new railway, 11 miles in length, received Parliamentary approval in 1910. It ran from Kirkby South Junction (already the starting point for the Great Northern's Leen Valley extension) in a north-easterly direction, through the southern part of Mansfield town, to Clipstone. Here there was a junction with the former Lancashire, Derbyshire & East Coast line (described in Chapter 10), serving en route the Mansfield, Rufford and Clipstone

Mansfield Central station in the 1930s. (Stations UK, Southport)

collieries, which were expected to produce three million tons of coal a year.

Passenger services, run by the Great Central (it had woken up late in the day to the potential for the new railway) on behalf of the Mansfield Railway, were provided at a new station, Mansfield Central, which had wooden platforms. The line continued through the eastern part of Mansfield on high embankments and girder bridges. Passenger trains ran south-wards from here to Kirkby South Junction and then via the Great Northern's Leen Valley line to Nottingham Victoria. Initially there were three trains each way a day, all connecting at Nottingham Victoria with Great Central expresses to London Marylebone. By 1939 there were 14 trains a day between Mansfield Central and Nottingham Victoria (12 in the other direction) and for a time in the 1930s the Leeds–Bournemouth express took this route. Between Mansfield Central and Kirkby South Junction there were stations at Sutton-in-Ashfield Central and Kirkby-in-Ashfield Central. After the Second World War the stations, particularly Mansfield Central, were looking somewhat dilapidated, and the regular service (eight northbound and seven southbound in 1955) between Mansfield and Nottingham Victoria was not being well patronised. All three stations closed for regular passenger services on 2nd January 1956, though during the summer months of that year seaside excursion trains continued to call there. The line had carried regular passenger services for only 39 years.

Mansfield Central station was demolished in 1972 and it is now difficult to trace any signs of the route through the town.

10
Lines North And East
Of Nottingham

*The Lancashire, Derbyshire & East
Coast Railway
Saxondale Junction to Stathern
Bottesford to Newark
Retford to Lincoln*

*An LNWR 2-4-0 Jumbo locomotive at the Nottingham London Road Low
Level station in 1905. (A. Shaw, courtesy of Nottingham City Council Leisure
and Community Services Central Library Local Studies Library)*

The Lancashire, Derbyshire & East Coast Railway

Robin Hood and Maid Marian were married in the parish church of Edwinstowe in the very heart of Sherwood Forest, within walking distance of the Major Oak, which is one of Nottinghamshire's favourite attractions, a huge ancient oak tree said to date from Robin Hood's time. Today tourists flock to Edwinstowe, where they can visit the Sherwood Forest Visitor Centre and the Sherwood Forest Country Park, as well as craft workshops and souvenir shops. Even 100 years ago, when the railway came to the village, its builders were aware of its potential, and Edwinstowe station was generously proportioned with extra platforms to receive the expected day-trippers (though the usual word then was 'excursionists').

The station at Edwinstowe in the heart of Sherwood Forest. It was generously proportioned in the hope of attracting excursion traffic, but this never materialised in the numbers hoped for. (Stations UK, Southport)

The viaduct which takes the LD&ECR route across the River Trent is still in place, though the railway lines now end at the High Marnham power station just short of the river. (Judy Kingscott)

But the line that came through Edwinstowe, as was so often the case in Nottinghamshire, was built primarily to tap into coal traffic, with passengers only as a secondary consideration. It was the ambitiously-named Lancashire, Derbyshire & East Coast Railway, which crosses Nottinghamshire from west to east and did run passenger trains from 1896 to 1955, but has now reverted to the status of purely a freight line.

Despite this independent railway company's initial plan to build a coast-to-coast line (from Warrington on the Manchester Ship Canal to Sutton-on-Sea, where new docks were to be built), only the section between Chesterfield (in Derbyshire) and Lincoln was actually ever laid down. This stretch, which was opened in 1896, enters Nottinghamshire between Langwith Junction and Shirebrook, north of Mansfield, and runs west to east through an area known (because so many ducal families had

134

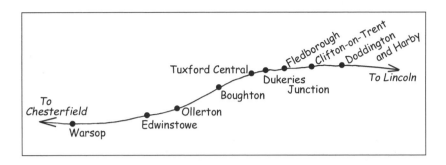

great houses there) as The Dukeries. For that reason it was often known as the Dukeries line.

The Midland Railway quickly reached an agreement with the new line to operate local passenger trains between Mansfield and Edwinstowe, and in 1897 they introduced their Nottingham to Heysham (the port for steamers for Ireland) service.

Ollerton station in 1954.

135

Tuxford Central station. (Priestley No. 108)

But the competition for the traffic between Sheffield, Nottingham and London at the start of the 20th century became fiercer than ever, with the Great Northern and Great Central co-operating to challenge the Midland Railway. A big blow to the Midland Railway was the acquisition of the LD&ECR by the Great Central Railway in 1907.

Stations in Nottinghamshire on this line were at Warsop, Edwinstowe, Ollerton, Boughton, Tuxford Central, Dukeries Junction, Fledborough, Clifton-on-Trent and Doddington & Harby. Passenger numbers were always disappointing and the stations closed to passengers in 1955 and 1956, except for some holiday excursions which continued into the 1960s.

The line is now used for freight only as far as the High Marnham power station, on the banks of the River Trent. Eastwards from here the tracks have been taken up, but the splendid viaduct that carried the line over the river is still in place, even if vegetation is growing over the trackbed. East of the Trent sections of the embankment are missing. The last section, the six miles from Harby to Lincoln, has been developed as a cycle route, part of the Sustrans National Cycle network.

136

Saxondale Junction to Stathern

Trains still run between Grantham and Nottingham on the line originally built by the Ambergate, Nottingham, Boston & Eastern Junction Railway, and later owned by the Great Northern (see Chapter 3). The majority of the stations are also still open, even if they are now mostly unmanned halts. However, some key branch lines from the Grantham–Nottingham line have closed.

One of these is the link between Saxondale Junction, near Bingham, to Stathern Junction, from where trains could continue south by joining the line from Bottesford to Melton Mowbray. This line, uniquely for Nottinghamshire, was jointly owned and run by the Great Northern Railway and the London & North Western Railway. Pre-Grouping the latter was certainly one of the country's major railway undertakings, but it had comparatively little presence in the East Midlands, except for

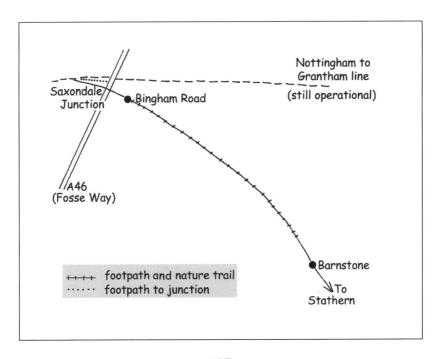

The LNWR goods depot at Manvers Street, Nottingham, is still a serviceable structure, although now cut off from any rail connection, and used for other purposes. The ramp on the right was up to the cattle dock. (Author)

Northampton. It did, however, have running rights over Great Northern lines, and this enabled it to operate the Northampton–Nottingham service (see Chapter 3).

Goods traffic was always important to the early railway companies, and the LNWR found it needed to have its own handling centre in Nottingham. It therefore created a short stretch of line leaving the Great Northern line at Trent Lane to a terminus at a purpose-built goods depot at Manvers Street, Nottingham. This major depot opened without ceremony, though a report in May 1887 in the *Nottingham Evening Post* suggested there was also a plan to open a passenger station. This, it seems, was never the intention, and would have upset the LNWR's relationship with the Great Northern.

Returning to our consideration of the Saxondale Junction to Stathern line, it is in fact possible to view where it started. From a

138

The Bingham Road station house, now a private residence. Our photograph was taken with the kind permission of the owner. (Judy Kingscott)

lay-by (SK 690400) on the western side of the A46 Leicester to Lincoln road (the Fosse Way) a signed footpath follows the line of the trackbed as far as the former junction. In the opposite direction, unfortunately, the embankment has been removed and new estates have spread out from the small town of Bingham to cover the route. However, the line of the trackbed can be picked up again from Nottingham Road in Bingham (SK 696395).

There was once a station where the line crossed Nottingham Road, the station being called Bingham Road, but this closed in 1951. Only the station house, now a private residence, remains.

South-east of Nottingham Road the old trackbed has been developed as a linear walkway and nature trail, an amenity much valued by Bingham residents. Indeed, by using the Ordnance Survey Landranger map no 129, practically the whole of the trackbed lying in Nottinghamshire, except for a ¾ mile section north of Barnstone, can still be traced.

Barnstone was the site of the other Nottinghamshire station on

The linear footpath and nature trail proceeding southwards out of Bingham goes under this high beautifully constructed masonry bridge ...

... and continues into the countryside, with even farm access bridges still intact. (Judy Kingscott)

this line. This closed to passengers in 1953 and then to goods in 1962, when the whole northern section of the line itself was closed. South from Barnstone the line ran straight, climbing steadily into Leicestershire and Stathern Junction.

Bottesford to Newark

The Great Northern Bottesford to Newark line ran from a junction with the Nottingham to Grantham line at Bottesford, more or less following the course of the River Devon, to Newark where it joined the East Coast main line. The branch opened in 1878 and closed in April 1987. There was only one station between Bottesford and Newark, and that was at the village of Cotham, which was more or less the halfway point. Cotham

141

Cotham station in 1954, at the end of its 85 year life. (Stations UK, Southport)

station opened for passengers on 14th April 1879, and closed on 11th September 1939, eight days after the outbreak of the Second World War. It remained open for goods until February 1964. The station buildings were later demolished.

The East Coast main line, pride of the Great Northern Railway, is still open and remains a major route between London and Scotland. Only stopping services have been discontinued, and stations such as Crow Park (closed to passengers in 1958) have disappeared from the railway map.

Retford to Lincoln

In north-east Nottinghamshire there was a Great Central Railway branch line, opened in 1850, from Retford to Lincoln. This is still open for freight traffic as far as Cottam power station (like High Marnham close to the River Trent) but the passenger stations at Leverton and Cottam (not to be confused with the Cotham

142

Cottam station, date unknown, but possibly in the 1960s, after closure of the station to passengers, even if the station seems to be still maintained. (Henry Priestley, by courtesy of Nottingham City Council Leisure and Community Services Central Library Local Studies Library)

Leverton station. (Henry Priestley, by courtesy of Nottingham City Council Leisure and Community Services Central Library Local Studies Library)

mentioned above) closed in 1959. One reason for closure was that expensive repairs would be needed on Torksey viaduct.

So many branch lines closed, so many little stations are no more. It takes a leap of imagination, now that private cars can take us wherever we want with comparative ease, to appreciate how utterly dependent rural communities once were on the railway. Village stations such as Cottam or Cotham were not just a couple of platforms and a booking office, they were the gateway to the greater world.

Conclusion

The Ordnance Survey maps for Nottinghamshire have the words 'Dismantled Railway' more frequently than those of any other county, because of the decline of the coal industry. It was that industry which had made Nottinghamshire such a centre for competition between rival railway companies, and led to considerable duplication of lines.

But Nottinghamshire is also the scene of new rail-based initiatives. The opening of the Robin Hood Line, mentioned in Chapter 7, and the creation of a brand-new Nottingham tramway system rank among the most important recent public transport developments in the country.

The last of the traditional trams had run in Nottingham in 1938. There had then been a gap of 66 years, till the new Nottingham Express Transit service opened for passenger service on 9th March 2004. The first stage links Nottingham's surviving railway system, centred on the Midland station, with the outlying town of Hucknall to the north. Outside the city the line runs on reserved track alongside an existing railway line (6 miles), but from the outskirts to the centre (for 2½ miles) it also threads through narrow streets to serve the Old Market Square.

So far there is just this one main line. A branch goes off to serve the large park-and-ride facility at Phoenix Park, built on the site of the old Cinderhill Colliery, which in Nottingham's railway past was served by the Derbyshire Extension. South of the Old Market Square the line reaches Midland station on a replacement viaduct, which follows more or less the same alignment as the old Great Central line running into what was once Victoria station. At the start and end of their journeys the trams wait on the last three remaining blue-brick arches of the old viaduct that

145

once carried Great Central trains over the Midland station.

Originally it was planned that the line between Basford and Hucknall would run along the existing railway tracks, now used for the Robin Hood Line, but this was not found to be feasible and the tram route now runs alongside the railway. To many Nottingham citizens this duplication of new public transport facilities does not seem to represent rationality in overall planning.

Further extensions to the tram system are at the planning and consultation stage. They include lines west to Chilwell and Clifton and a new viaduct, which will be on the alignment of the old Great Central Railway, to cross the railway tracks at Nottingham Midland station. There are as yet no proposals to go east on the route of the old Suburban Railway.

One wonders what Dr Beeching would be thinking if he were alive today. Here we are in the 21st century, and at great expense we are rebuilding facilities such as viaducts when serviceable constructions on the same alignments were closed and demolished as a result of his famous report. It highlights

Rail and tramway run side by side at Bulwell station. (Author)

146

A new viaduct has had to be built for the Nottingham tramway approximately on the route of the demolished Great Central viaduct. (Rodger Smith)

the two main defects of the Beeching approach. The first that it failed to foresee road traffic congestion, which would switch the emphasis back from individually driven cars and commercial vehicles (surely the most labour-intensive, energy-intensive and space-intensive form of transport) to mass transit systems. The second was that it failed to take account of the potential value of the wonderfully engineered infrastructure that was already in place.

What our generation, and future generations, must ensure is that what survives of the infrastructure represented by our

147

Viewing the lots before the start of a Sheffield Railwayana auction.
(Judy Kingscott)

railway heritage is not heedlessly thrown away. Even when it is obviously uneconomic to run that socially useful and environmentally friendly form of transport called a railway, there are other uses to which station buildings and trackbeds can be put.

But while a new generation of planners and passengers is discovering the advantages of railed transport, there are many people who have never forgotten them, people who value the great railway achievements, particularly those of the Victorian and Edwardian ages, when everyone, from royalty to paupers, took the train. There are two steadily growing movements, with a large amount of overlap between them. One is the heritage railway movement, which is re-creating old lines and running trains again, often drawn by historic steam locomotives. The other is the interest in railway memorabilia.

To a large extent Nottinghamshire has missed out on heritage railway developments. The Nottingham Transport Heritage Centre at Ruddington is a comparatively small affair, compared with the Midland Railway Centre at Butterley, just a few miles over the Derbyshire border, or with the Great Central Railway running between Loughborough (just inside Leicestershire) and the city of Leicester. But, as we have seen, there are plans afoot to connect the Ruddington centre with the Great Central Railway at Loughborough. Then indeed there will be reflections of past glories within Nottinghamshire, and perhaps the overgrown wilderness of East Leake station will return to functional operation, and see passengers embarking and disembarking once again.

The interest in railway memorabilia is not only growing, it can rival any other sector of the antiques business for expertise and excitement. The regular auctions that are held in various parts of the country present for sale everything from cast iron trackside signs to hand-lamps, from pre-war railway posters to refreshment room spoons stamped LMS or LNER. But the most valued items are station signs and locomotive nameplates.

In the 1950s British Railways introduced a standard type of station sign to which they gave the name 'totem'. These signs, with their Sans Gill lettering and regional colours, were much more attractive than anything that came before, or after. There are probably about 500 dedicated totem collectors in the country, and about another 500 occasional collectors. A totem in good condition will sell from between £500 to £2,000, though rare ones will fetch much more. But these prices are chickenfeed compared to what enthusiasts will pay for genuine locomotive nameplates. Your author recalls vividly his first-ever visit to the regular auction known as Sheffield Railwayana, and the tense atmosphere – between bids you could hear the proverbial pin drop – when the nameplate 'Cock o' the North' was sold for a record £54,500.

The proprietor and auctioneer of Sheffield Railwayana, and one of the country's leading experts in the value of railway memorabilia, is Ian Wright. When asked whether he was worried that when the last generation who remembered steam had passed away the market for memorabilia would collapse, he replied: 'You forget that new generations are coming up who have been brought up to revere steam engines. Thank goodness for Thomas the Tank Engine! Railways are an essential part of the British psyche.'

149

Those were the days! The Princess Coronation class locomotive 46251, carrying the proud name of 'City of Nottingham', emerges bright and clean after receiving special attention at Annesley Locomotive Depot. (Henry Priestley, courtesy of Nottingham City Council Leisure and Community Services Central Library Local Studies Library)

150

So whether railways are revived, or turned into cycle tracks or monuments, or are only preserved in photographs or memorabilia, or even books such as this one, one thing is certain – in Nottinghamshire as elsewhere – lost railways will never be completely lost.

Bibliography

Aldworth, Colin *The Nottingham and Melton Railway 1872–1990* (Colin Aldworth, 1990)

Anderson, Paul and Cupit, Jack *An Illustrated History of Mansfield's Railways* (Irwell Press, Clophill, Bedfordshire, 2000)

Anderson, P. Howard *Forgotten Railways – The East Midlands* (David & Charles, 1985)

Beckett, John (ed) *A Centenary History of Nottingham* (Manchester University Press, 1997)

Best, Stephen *Railway Stations in Nottinghamshire* (provisional listing produced for the Nottingham Local Studies Library, 1978)

Biddle, Gordon *Britain's Historic Railway Buildings* (Oxford University Press, 2003)

Birks, J. and Coxon, P. *Account of Railway Development in the Nottinghamshire Coalfield* (typescript, 1949; bound copy in Nottingham Central Library Local Studies Library)

Brazier, S. R. Hammond and Waterman, S.R. *A New Geography of Nottingham* (Trent Polytechnic, Nottingham, 1984)

Cupit, J. and Taylor, W. *The Lancashire, Derbyshire & East Coast Railway* (Oakwood Press, 1966)

Durose, Ashley R. *Railways Remembered: Basford & Bulwell, 1818-1967* (Happy Walking International Limited, Matlock, 1999)

Hawkins, Mac *The Great Central, Then and Now* (BCA by arrangement with David & Charles, 1992)

Henshaw, Alfred *The Great Northern Railway in the East Midlands, The Erewash Valley Lines, Pinxton Branch, Awsworth–Illkeston, Heanor and Stanton Branches* (Railway Correspondence and Travel Society, 2000)

Henshaw, Alfred *The Great Northern Railway in the East Midlands, Nottingham–Grantham, Bottesford–Newark, Melton Mowbray, the Leicester Line and Ironstone Branches* (Railway Correspondence and Travel Society, 2003)

Henshaw, Alfred *The Great Northern Railway in the East Midlands, Colwick Yards, Nottingham London Road, Gedling, Basford* (Railway Correspondence and Travel Society, 1999)

Lund, Brian *Nottinghamshire Railway Stations On Old Picture Postcards* (Reflections of a Bygone Age, Keyworth, Nottinghamshire, 1991)

Marshall, John *The Nottingham Suburban Railway* (in *British Railway Journal*, no 14, Christmas 1986)

Simmons, Jack *The Victorian Railway* (Thames and Hudson, 1991)

Vanags, John *The Mansfield and Pinxton Railway* (Old Mansfield Society, 2000)

Vanns, Michael A. *Rail Centres: Nottingham* (Ian Allan, 1993)

Vanns, Michael A. *The Railways of Newark-on-Trent* (Oakwood Press, Usk, Monmouthshire, 1999)

Vinter, Jeff *Railway Walks, LMS* (Alan Sutton Publishing Ltd, 1990)

Welbourn, Nigel *Lost Lines: LMR* (Ian Allan, 1994)

Wilson, J.P. *The Development of Nottingham's Railways* (Nottingham Civic Society)

Woodward, N.E. *A Half-forgotten Midland Byway* (in *LMS News*, October 1983/March 1984)

Wright, Gordon *Nottinghamshire Steam Railways in the 1960s* (Reflections of a Bygone Age, Keyworth, Nottinghamshire, 2002)

There are also a number of websites that deal with Nottinghamshire railways. These include:

www.nottm-melton-railway.co.uk A site maintained by Colin Aldworth, devoted entirely to the Nottingham to Melton line.

www.leytransporti12.com/nott.htm Nottingham railway archive.

www.homepage.ntlworld.com/nick.willis A site, created by a young enthusiast, dedicated to Nottingham Victoria station.

www.leverton.org/tunnels/nottingham Information on Nottinghamshire railway routes.

www.railwayarchive.org.uk A national railway website.

www.nottinghamrail.com A site devoted entirely to railways in the city.

www.thewoodheadsite.org.uk/gcrs The site of the Great Central Railway Society.

INDEX